THE WEEK WITH CHRIST

THE WEEK WITH CHRIST

Liturgy For The Apostolate

EMERIC A. LAWRENCE, O.S.B.

FIDES

SOUTH BEND CHICAGO MONTREAL PARIS

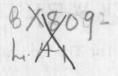

TO MY PARENTS

CONTENTS

CONTENTS

(Continued)

CONTENTS
(Continued)

VIII

INTRODUCTION

The Catholic Church is the permanent incarnation of Christ. When the Word was made flesh in the womb of the virgin Mary, the incarnation was only begun. It was to continue until the end of time, until the final coming of Christ. The whole purpose of Christ's coming was to make of the human family "a chosen people, a kingly priesthood, a holy nation." The Church would grow like a mustard seed from the tiniest of beginnings into a great organism covering the entire world. But the growth would be gradual and progressive. It would follow closely the development of the world itself. In apostolic times, the Church followed the roads of Rome. In feudal Europe, it patterned itself after the social structure of an emerging Western civilization. In the time of the discoveries of America and Asia, she sailed with Columbus and Vasco da Gamma in their ships. Today, the Church takes to the air in an effort to reach all men.

Not only does the Church incarnate the world extensively and horizontally but intensively and vertically. She incarnates not only human generations but also their peculiar characteristics. If the twentieth century is democratic and if the democratic ideal is a genuine human growth, then the Church, too, without necessarily abandoning her authoritarian principle, will lay more stress on the equality of all men, which she has preached from her very inception. "I am come not to be ministered unto but to minister." "Whatever you do unto the least of my brethern, you do unto me." The world will find in the Church the vital energy to make a democracy a true equality, an equality that does not reduce mankind to a common denominator but raises it to new heights, to divine heights.

In this light, the modern effort towards a fuller participation in the worship of the Church and a wider participation in her apostolate must be seen. The renewed interest in the Liturgy and in Catholic Action reveal the laity coming of age, becoming adult within the Church and seeking to share more fully in the whole life of the Church. The liturgical movement and the Catholic Action movement within the Church are manifestations of genuine growth and, I am sure, will find greater acceptance in the Church, as they begin to reveal real life and vitality.

The liturgy and the apostolate are not two separate movements. If they remain separate, they will die. The liturgy must not confine itself to the altar, for liturgy is life and must necessarily include all of life. The layman must offer his life and his station in life, his world, to God. Likewise, the present interest in Catholic Action cannot confine itself to one mere segment of life but must extend itself to all of life. The lay apostle must begin to see that active participation in the liturgy is a formative institution for the apostolate. One cannot possibly be an apostle of the liturgy without at the same time being in-

X

terested in the apostolate, nor can he possibly engage in Catholic Action without being interested in the liturgy. Living in Christ means that we go to God in the Liturgy and to man in the apostolate. Love of God and love of neighbor are one and the same commandment.

For this reason, the *Week With Christ* by Father Lawrence is a work of great promise and of great need. For the layman, the Mass is his principal means of formation. The liturgy must be the great teacher as well as the fountain of divine life. Like the Samaritan woman at Jacob's well, we stand to draw a new life not from the well but from the very person of Christ Who continues His life in the Church. "If thou didst know the gift of God and Who He is Who speaks to thee, thou wouldst have asked Him and He would give thee living water." This volume will help us draw from that source for a richer life.

— Louis J. Putz, C.S.C.

PREFACE

These explanations of the Sunday Masses had their beginning as far back as 1940, when they came out in mimeograph form for the students of St. John's University and later for the chaplains of the armed forces who desired to receive them. During the past year they were taken up again and entirely revised. The author's main purpose now is to show how the Liturgical Year can be a magnificent source of inspiration for the spiritual well-being and development of modern lay apostles. To Christianize one has to be Christlike, or at least, want very badly to be Christlike. There is no better source of Christlike holiness than an understanding and loving sharing in the Liturgy. And therefore, "the most pressing duty of Christians is to live the liturgical life, and increase and cherish its supernatural spirit" (Pius XII, *Mediator Dei*, par. 197).

Of course the book is not meant exclusively for lay apostles. It is true that Catholic Action is for the laity. But every priest or religious who is close to our Lord's heart and mind will want to ally his or her thinking to what is closest to that heart — the spread of His kingdom on earth. Father Daniélou puts this very strongly : "Christianity is catholic by definition, that is, it embraces the world. A Christian spirituality that is not fundamentally oriented towards the building up of the total Mystical Body is not a Catholic spirituality" (*The Salvation of the Nations*, page 1).

Therefore it is the author's hope that the following pages will help to form apostolic mentalities in *all* readers, and that priests, Sisters, and all the aged, ill, and otherwise occupied lay men and women who are prevented from taking an active part in the apostolate will be inspired to offer daily prayers and sacrifices for their brethren who are spending themselves for Christ.

There is much talk these days about contemplation and mental prayer, and that is most encouraging. But there might be some misunderstanding about the true purpose of contemplation. It is necessary for us, not primarily because we need it in order to be truly human, but most of all because God is God, the supreme Value above all values. The Liturgy is contemplation of God by Christ and the Church, His Mystical Body. It is Christ's prayer of praise, of gratitude, of atonement, of petition constantly going up to the Father.

In that Christly prayer and worship we are privileged to participate — all of us together. It is social prayer, the prayer of a family, the family of God, which requires whole-hearted sharing on the part of all the members. If we as members of this family (and its visible counterpart, the parish) are primarily concerned about God's glory, as Christ was, we will not have to worry about ourselves, our needs, even our apostolate. God understands about these things better than we do ourselves. Praying Christ's prayer with understanding and desire is the best way to bring God into the range of our "experience." As He spoke to Moses out of the burning bush, so does He communicate Himself to us through the texts of the Sacred Liturgy. To experience God's nearness is to love Him. It is to know Him as He is and to be filled more and more with the desire to do what He wants us to do. And this gives the correct orientation to our apostolic work. For the purpose of the apostolate, in the words of Father Lochet, "is not to give God to man so that man will be happier, but to give man to God so that He will be more loved" *(La Vie Spirituelle*, November 1948, page 387).

To make God more loved is the author's desire, and it is also his excuse for the certain amount of moralizing that will be evident. Following Christ's life as it is re-enacted in the Liturgical Year must inevitably cause us to contrast our shortcomings with His perfection. This contrasting has been favored in the hope that critical self-examination will produce repentance and then love, the basis of conversion to Christ.

The author would like to see the book used as a handmaid to the missal. Certainly it is not intended as a substitute for the missal and for the reader's personal effort to plunge into the depths of the texts to get at their profound meaning and to make it his own. Many of the Mass texts are quoted verbatim ; and at the end of each explanation several texts are listed which, if concentrated on, may help the reader retain the main thoughts of the Mass during the week to the end that his will truly be weeks with and in Christ.

It would be a serious omission not to mention those authors who have provided inspiration and ideas for this work : Pius Parsch *(Le Guide dans L'Année Litur-gique)* ; Dame Emiliana Loehr, O.S.B. *(The Year of Our Lord)* ; C.C. Martindale, S.J. *(The Prayers of the Missal)* ; and Monsignor Martin B. Hellriegel *(Vine and Branches)*.

Finally, the author wishes to express his gratitude to his many confreres and friends who have helped this book along its way to publication, in particular : The Right Reverend Abbot Alcuin Deutsch, Fathers God-frey Diekmann, and Michael Marx of St. John's Ab-bey ; Mr. and Mrs. Emerson Hynes, the Young Chris-tian Students Groups of St. John's University and St. John's Preparatory School, and the members of his own family.

St. John's Abbey
Collegeville, Minnesota
Feast of the Assumption of the Blessed Virgin,
1950

THE LITURGICAL YEAR

For the Apostles, Christ and His living among them was actuality. There was nothing unreal or past history about it. He was there. They saw with their eyes and touched with their hands the Word of Life. With Him they lived a most intimate family life, sharing with Him His joys, sorrows, sacrifice, His humiliation and His glorification.

We have no cause to envy them. There are apostles and apostles, but there is only one Christ. And there is only one life lived by Christ. *He lives that life now in His Church, His Mystical Body,* His new presence among men. We do not see Him as the first apostles did, but if we are to believe His word ("I am with you all days..."), He is as really present to us as He was to them. "Come, follow Me," He says to us as He once said to St. Matthew.

This is not irresponsible talk or mere wishful thinking. Listen to Pius XII : "The Liturgical Year, devotedly fostered and accompanied by the Church, is not a cold and lifeless representation of the events of the past, or a simple and bare record of a former age. *It is rather Christ Himself who is ever living in His Church.* Here He con-

1

tinues that journey of immense mercy which He lovingly began in His mortal life, going about doing good, with the design of bringing men to know His mysteries and in a way to live by them" *(Mediator Dei,* par. 165).

OUR PART

The Liturgical Year, then, is mainly Christ's year. It is His normal way of saving us now and keeping us saved. But it is more than that. It is our year and our work, too. We have a part in it just as the apostles had, and Christ depends on us now just as He depended on the apostles then. From Christ's living with His apostles in Palestine there came forth the conversion and salvation of the world. Why not the conversion of our world from our living with Christ this year, and the next, and the next ?

We know we cannot do it alone, this Christ-like work given into our hands. But we know it has to be done. Like it or not, we are apostles, consecrated to the apostolate both by the touch of Christ in Baptism and Confirmation and by the call of Christ's Vicars, the Popes. "You have not chosen me, but I have chosen you... that you should go and should bring forth fruit" (John 16: 16).

We cannot do Christ's work alone, but we can do it with Him and with His help. In the Church Year, He not only fills us with His love for the Father, His dedication to the will of the Father, but also with His hunger for souls and His desire to consecrate the world to the Father's glory. He also gives us the zeal and energy to

2

continue that divine program in our own environments. But we must want Him and His help. Only our free choice can save us and through us save our world.

We can make that free choice by penetrating with understanding, faith, and love into the changeable texts of the missal and (if possible) the Divine Office as these carry us along the way of the next fifty-two Sundays. These texts contain Christ's mind, His vision, His saving will. We must eat and drink at this source. If we do we shall be filled, because the source is Christ, the "fountain of living waters."

ADVENT

If Christ is ever living in His Church, we may wonder what He wants us to think about and to do during these four weeks preceding His Nativity. Obviously, He wants us to prepare ourselves for His coming, or more exactly, His *comings*. The texts of Advent tell us plainly that this holy season is not only a preparation for Christ's coming to us at Christmas, but above all, it is a preparation for the second coming of Christ in judgment at the end of time.

"Great Judge of all! in the last day
When friends shall fail and foes combine,
Be present then with us, we pray,
To guard us with Thine arm divine" (Vespers hymn).

This may seem difficult to grasp: that Advent prepares us for Christ's coming in judgment. But why did He come in the first place ? What was at stake for us—years or eons, time or eternity? Short passing well-being for men now, or everlasting happiness in union with the God of all desires? This life with its work, joy, love, sorrow is important. But it ends. So are Christmas, Epiphany, Good Friday, and Easter important. But one

Liturgical Year succeeds another, and this life's Liturgical Years will be gone forever after the Last Day.

Therefore, our Lord tells us, think about My final coming in connection with My coming this year at Christmas. "And then they will see the Son of Man coming upon a cloud with great power and majesty. But when these things begin to come to pass, look up, and lift up your heads, because your redemption is at hand" (Gospel, First Sunday of Advent). Our Redemption is at hand now. We stand at Redemption at every holy Mass and there give our personal consent to it. But we shall come into its full possession only when Christ comes again either at our death or on the Last Day.

But we are living in this world now. We have to sanctify this world. Christ is concerned about us in this life too. Are we weary of our daily cross? Is the task of being a true Christian discouraging and unfruitful? No matter what our spiritual condition is, Advent is the answer to our heart's desire: Advent with its nourishing truth and life, its hope, its assurance of final success in life and in the apostolate. "All ye who thirst, come to the waters: seek the Lord while He can be found" (Antiphon at Lauds). *We need Advent.* And now we have it. "MARANATHA... COME, LORD JESUS!" This Advent prayer of the early Christians is our prayer now. He can come at the end, but we need Him now. We must be filled with His vision, His love for souls, His knowledge of our God and desire for the glory of God. Come, Lord, and do not delay!

"Bedew us, heaven from above;
Ye clouds, rain down the Just One."

5

FIRST SUNDAY OF ADVENT

THE ESSENTIAL PRAYER

"To Thee, O Lord, have I lifted up my soul : in Thee, O My God, I put my trust; let me not be ashamed. Neither let my enemies laugh at me; for none of them that wait on Thee shall be confounded. Show, O Lord, Thy ways to me, and teach me Thy paths" (Introit).

In this way do we start our year of contemplation, our year of grace. This is the prayer of mankind of every age, the prayer of the creature in the presence of the Creator, of the sinner in the presence of the All-Holy One. Here at the beginning of a new year of grace and growth for our Church and ourselves, her members, we Thy creatures, but also Thy sons and daughters, recognize Thee as our God. We turn to Thee with confidence that Thou wilt heal us. But we are weak and inclined to sin. We live in a world that lives without Thee. Let us not be ashamed of our calling, nor let our enemies laugh at us. Show us Thy ways and teach us Thy paths in this world. And help us to remember this beginning throughout the year, throughout our lives. "Stir us Thy power, we beseech Thee, O Lord, and come: that from

6

the threatening dangers of our sins we may be rescued by Thy protection, and saved by Thy deliverance" (Collect).

In the Epistle Christ through St. Paul lectures us firmly about keeping first things first. He vividly points out the dangers we face on the path to God that we pray for in the Introit. "It is now the hour for us to rise from sleep, because now our salvation is nearer than when we came to believe. The night is far advanced ; the day is at hand. Let us therefore lay aside the works of darkness and put on the armor of light" (Epistle). Our Lord means that we are to rise from the sleep of forgetfulness of God and of our duties to Him and our neighbor. He thinks of the sleep of sloth and neglect of prayer, the sleep of materialism that makes us try to live as though He did not exist.

This is the sleep that weakens our resistance to our greatest enemy — the enemy of growth in grace for us and for the Church, the enemy of present peace and of final salvation. That enemy is sin. Sin is the work of darkness. Growth in consciousness of God's presence around us and in us is to walk honestly as in the day. "Let us walk becomingly as in the day, not in revelry and drunkenness, not in debauchery and wantonness, not in strife and jealousy. But PUT ON THE LORD JESUS CHRIST" (Epistle). Following Christ in the Church Year by feeding on and living into these Mass texts will be to put on the Lord Jesus Christ ; it will be to make our own His prayer, His worship, His joy, His mind. And with the mind of Christ in us, revelry, wantonness, strife and jealousy will have no place in our lives.

7

But we know ourselves and our weaknesses, and Christ does too. We need more than lecturing. Therefore He follows the Epistle with His own description of the Last Judgment. "There will be signs in the sun and moon and stars, and upon the earth distress of nations... men fainting for fear and for expectation of the things that are coming on the world ; for the powers of heaven will be shaken. And then they will see the Son of Man coming upon a cloud with great power and majesty" (Gospel). We do not know if we shall see that terrifying day. But we do know that death is coming to us, and after death, judgment. Are we ready for it ? For some death will mean eternal damnation, everlasting separation from our God. But if we heed Christ, if we live and love His prayer, the Liturgy, if we are apostolic as He was, then, when these things come to pass, we can lift up our heads, because our Redemption will be at hand.

And now we are ready for the Offertory of the Mass and the re-enacting of Christ's redeeming act. We must never stand at redemption empty-handed. What can we give to Christ's sacrifice ? "To Thee have I lifted up my soul: in Thee, O My God, I put my trust" (Offertory verse). The priest in our name offers up bread and wine to God. The bread and wine, we know, are symbols of ourselves — of our souls, our bodies, our life in the world, our work, our love, our trust. We say we offer all things. The proof of our sincerity is in our life during the week and during the whole year. "May these holy offerings, O Almighty God, cleanse us by their mighty power, and make us more pure to approach Him who is their Author" (Secret Prayer).

"The Lord will give goodness : and our earth shall yield her fruit" (Communion verse). This goodness and fruit will be Christ at Christmas, Christ in our lives, Christ in our apostolate ; but only on condition that we lift up our souls to God and keep them lifted up on the fifty-two pegs of this year's Masses.

FOOD FOR THE WAY

1. To Thee, O Lord, have I lifted up my soul : in Thee, O My God, I put my trust (Introit).
2. Show us, O Lord, Thy Mercy : and grant us Thy Salvation (Alleluia verse).
3. Lift up your heads, because your redemption is at hand (Gospel).

SECOND SUNDAY OF ADVENT

MORE ON ADVENT

Many of the texts of the Sunday Advent Masses are from the Old Testament prophets, texts which are expressive of deep yearning. But this does not mean that we are to go back in imagination to those pre-Christian times now. Remember the Holy Father's words : "The Liturgical Year is not a lifeless representation of the past." Of course it is good for us to make our own the longing desire of the just ones of the Old Testament. But it is much better and more practical to consider Advent in its present and future meaning *for us*.

Last Sunday St. Paul indicated our present vocation : "Put ye on the Lord Jesus Christ." We are not to put on Christ externally as we put on a coat. *We are to grow in union with Him.* This union in which we are to grow as we live with Him in the Church Year is a union of life and of love to the end that He will begin to take over in our lives and we will begin to think as He thinks and to love as He loves.

REASON FOR REJOICING

The spirit of the Advent Masses indicated that the Church is fully aware of her obligation to help us grow in oneness with Christ and thus to make us ready for that second coming of Jesus that we spoke of last week. The difference between the Church's thinking of the Last Judgment and ours is nicely developed in today's Mass. "Behold the Lord shall come to save the nations : and the Lord shall make the glory of His voice to be heard in the joy of your heart" (Introit). "Out of Sion the loveliness of His beauty : God shall come manifestly. Gather ye together His saints to Him" (Gradual). There is surely nothing sad or frightening about those texts... or about the alleluia verse : "I rejoiced at the things that were said to me : we shall go into the house of the Lord.

For the Church preparation for Christmas and for the Last Judgment are one and the same thing. So they must be for us. Longing and rejoicing. We will have reason for rejoicing not only on the last day but already now because all our lives we learn from Christ through His Church Year *to hope*. We learn to hope, and hope is given to us. In today's Epistle St. Paul, Christ, and the whole Church pray for us : "Now the God of hope fill you with all joy and peace in believing : that you may abound in hope and in the power of the Holy Ghost."

If there is one thing we need in life, and especially in the apostolate, it is hope. Hope comes mostly from a keen awareness of what we are and have and what we are for. We are members of Christ's Mystical Body — we have *His* Life in us : *"Christ in you, the hope of glory"* (Colossians 1 : 27). And what are we for ? We are to put on Christ, to grow in union with Him and our neighbor, grow in awareness of our union with Him, and to prepare others for a similar basis of hope.

CHRIST'S NEED FOR US

The Christian is a man with a cause, which is none other than the cause of Christ whom he strives to put on. He is therefore a man of hope. But he has to learn to act as a man of hope. So few of us have that awareness of, and enthusiasm for, our cause that we should have. We give in to gloom and pessimism when we do not notice results. Hence today's Collect was never more timely : "Stir up our hearts, O Lord, to prepare the ways of Thine only-begotten Son : that through His coming we may attain to serve Thee with purified minds." In other words we pray that we will have courage enough to make ready our own hearts for Christ's taking over at Christmas, so that thenceforward we may serve God in joy and hope, and with minds purified of excessive self-interest and self-love. There is hardly a better service of God than seeking to extend and intensify His Kingdom in ourselves and others.

And this brings us to the Gospel, which is about St. John the Baptist, Christ's Precursor. Historically our Lord had John go before Him to prepare the people for His coming. "This is he of whom it is written, 'Behold, I send my messenger before thy face, who shall make ready the way before thee. ' " It is not good psychology suddenly to overwhelm men with world-shattering truths. If Christ, who knew human psychology as we never shall, used John to go before Him and prepare hearts for His first coming, does He not need us to do the same work for Him today. This certainly is not the least of the present meanings of Advent for us.

What is the apostolate ? It is simply the conditioning of the soil of men's souls for the sowing of Christ's grace. Christ himself does the planting. "Behold, I send my messenger... who shall make ready thy way before thee." If we can understand that God was speaking not only about John but also about us, then we will rejoice as we go into the House of the Lord at the end of life, bringing with us the conquests inspired by "Christ in us, our hope of glory."

FOOD FOR THE WAY

1. Stir up our hearrts, O Lord, to prepare the ways of Thine only-begotten Son ; That through His coming we may serve Thee with purified minds. (Collect).
2. I rejoiced at the things that were said to me : we shall go into the house of the Lord (Alleluia verse).
3. Show us, O Lord, Thy mercy, and grant us Thy salvation (Offertory verse).

THIRD SUNDAY OF ADVENT

THE LORD IS NEAR

The moralizers can find a lot of things wrong with us and our world. They say that we are selfish, spoiled, immoral, and amoral ; that our age is characterized by fast living, furious activity, and the cult of conveniences. That, in short, ours is a Godless age that has even dared to empty the sacred feast of Christmas of its deep spiritual content. The moralizers are probably right in their diagnosis of our times. They are especially right in their uncovering the fear of thinking, the fear of living, the restless sense of insecurity and even despair under-lying our front of false gaity. Beneath our external finery we are a sick people, with not nearly enough psychiatrists on hand to care for us.

But poor old Mother Church seems entirely unaware of our sad condition. Or perhaps she is more aware than we realize. Perhaps she has more of a cure for us than the psychiatrists have. Today she cries out to us and to our world : "REJOICE IN THE LORD ALWAYS ; again I say, rejoice... HAVE NO ANXIETY" (Introit). Says our world : "Rejoice ? But the moralizers tell us that is just what is wrong with us. However, if you in-sist..."

14

The Church answers : "Rejoice *in the Lord !* Rejoice because the *Lord is near !*" Rejoicing in the Lord, rejoicing because He is near, may be a strange occupation for our world, but one thing to be said about our world is that it is ready to try anything... once. Only it has to be shown. That is where we come in. We Catholics have to realize that Christ is near in this and every Mass ; for in the Mass He reenacts for us the Sacrifice of the Cross in which He continues to draw us to Himself. And when He draws us to Himself, He is nearer than near : He is in us, and we can say with St. Paul : "Christ liveth in me." He lives in us so that "He can work in us the wonders of His salvation" (Secret prayer).

But the Lord is near in another way. His coming at Christmas is near, too, and that is something quite special. St. Paul gives an idea of what that Christmas coming can bring : "May the peace of Christ that surpasses all understanding guard your hearts and your minds in Christ Jesus, our Lord" (Epistle). Only Christ can bring that peace. His problem is getting into our hearts. Hearts full of fear, distrust, envy, hatred ; hearts interested only in self are like the inn St. Joseph tried to enter that first Christmas : there was no room. No room for Christ and the peace of God that surpasses all understanding.

ONE IN OUR MIDST

The Gospel tells what is wrong both with the world and the worriers : "There hath stood one in the midst

15

of you whom you do not know." We do not know that Christ is in us by grace, we forget all about "I am the vine, you are the branches." We do not know that our Mass is so powerful that it can "wonderfully work in us His salvation" (Secret). We do not know that Christ is in His Church, and that we can therefore make Christmas just as real and fruitful for us as for the Shepherds to whom angels announced great joy. We do not know that He is in our midst in His poor, that what we do to them we do to Him.

To sum it all up, we do not know Him because darkness has covered our faith. We have run after and adored the false god of selfish pride. We have tried to live without Christ and we are therefore groping in the shadows. But it is not too late, not as long as we can pray "O God, enlighten the darkness of our minds by the grace of Thy visitation" (Collect). "Stir up, O Lord, Thy might, and come : that Thou mayest save us" (Alleluia verse). Christ has really redeemed us already ; but it seems that His most difficult task is keeping us redeemed, saving us from ourselves, from the despair and discouragement we bring on ourselves when we forget and neglect Him, from the darkness of the night of suffering and fear that blot Him out of our lives even though He is in our very midst.

There stands One in our midst. He will be even more in our midst on Christmas. Karl Adam says : Christianity is consciousness of victory. The path on which we are to meet God is open. God is once and for all ours again, and we are His. Where Christ is there can be no anxiety. 'Why are ye fearful, O ye of little faith... ? Peace be with you, it is I, fear not' " (Orate

Fratres, Vol. 12, No. 1, p. 14). "SAY TO THE FAINT-HEARTED, TAKE COURAGE AND FEAR NOT: BEHOLD OUR GOD WILL COME AND WILL SAVE US" (Communion verse).

MAKE STRAIGHT THE WAY

But just longing for Christ to come to light up the darkness of our hearts is not enough. We must listen to and obey John the Baptist : "Do penance, repent, for the kingdom of heaven is as hand... Make the way of the Lord, make straight His paths" (Matthew 3:2-4).

St. John once said to the Pharisees: "Brood of vipers! who has shown you how to flee from the wrath to come? Bring forth fruit befitting repentance, and do not think within yourselves : 'We have Abraham for our father!... For even now the axe is laid to the root of the trees; every tree therefore that is not bringing forth good fruit is to be cut down and thrown into the fire" (Matthew 3:7-11).

Those are strong words, but good for us to hear, necessary for us to hear if we truly wish to prepare for Christ's coming to us. We too are often tempted to rely on our inheritance: "We are Catholics. We have the faith." St. John would bridle at our conceit and would say to us: "Repent! Do penance! Change your ways. Cleanse your hearts of self-love." The Ember Days are coming this week — days of fast and abstinence. We must deny ourselves and so test the sincerity of our Advent longing. Christ is coming. Are we prepared for Him? There is so little time. "We implore Thy mercy,

17

O Lord, that these Divine aids may help us to atone for sin and prepare for the coming Feast" (Postcommunion prayer).

FOOD FOR THE WAY

1. Rejoice in the Lord always; again I say, rejoice... The Lord is near (Introit).
2. Lord, Thou has blest Thy land: Thou hast turned away the captivity of Jacob: Thou hast forgiven the iniquity of Thy people (Offertory verse).
3. Behold our God will come and will save us (Communion verse).

FOURTH SUNDAY OF ADVENT

DESIRE

This is God's work, this Advent Liturgy. It is He who is trying to shape us up. He is near. "The Lord is nigh unto all them that call upon Him, to all that call upon Him in truth" (Gradual). The moment is at hand. The marvellous event is about to occur. To key us up to proper spiritual readiness, this Mass brings to focus all the longing aspirations of Mary, John the Baptist, and the Prophet Isaias, and she permits us to share those aspirations. The Mass is full of expectancy and desire.

There are many forms of desire: the voiceless longing of the parched land for rain; the desire of the hungry and thirsty man for food and water; the desire of the human heart for love; and yearning of everyman for change. Only the Liturgy is able to give word and shape to what underlies all these desires — man's hunger for God: "DROP DOWN DEW, YE HEAVENS, FROM ABOVE, AND LET THE CLOUDS RAIN DOWN THE JUST ONE; LET THE EARTH BE OPENED AND BUD FORTH A SAVIOR" (Introit).

And only the liturgy is capable of satisfying that desire. "Behold a Virgin shall conceive, and bring forth

19

a son; and His name shall be called Emmanuel" (Communion verse). Emmanuel means "God-with-us." Mary bore Him to us and to our world. He is still God-with-us in the Church, in the Mass, in the Church Year where "He continues that journey of immense mercy which He lovingly began in His mortal life, going about doing good" (Pius XII).

MARY AND ISAIAS

"Hail Mary, full of grace: the Lord is with thee: blessed art thou among women and blessed is the fruit of thy womb" (Offertory verse)! How does our looking forward to Christmas compare with Mary's eager joyful longing ? We must try to imagine what her feelings and thoughts were. She had been in most perfect possession of the Savior of the world for nine months. He was all hers. But she longed for the moment when she could bring Him forth and give Him to the world so that He might belong to us as well.

Mary presides over the Offertory of this and every Mass. Next to her Son she is the most perfect of givers. She presides over this and every Christmas. She must preside over our life, for she is the perfect type of the lay apostle. With her we must long for Christ's birth in us so that we can offer Him, and ourselves with Him, to our world and after that the world and ourselves to God.

Isaias foresees the punishment that will come upon his people: "Lo, the city of the Holy One is made a desert, Sion has become a desert. Jerusalem, waste and desolate" (Advent Song). This prophecy could be true of any people which refuses to accept this Savior. A desert is a frightening place, whether it be spiritual or geographical, whether it be in the Old Testament or the New. There is no joy there, no hope, no moisture, but only fear, death, drifting sands, and erosion.

And that is much of our world today, this world without its God. This world needs the rain of Divine Life. It needs Christmas. We individually need Christmas, and so we pray: "Stir up Thy might, we beseech Thee, O Lord, and come; accompany us with great power, so that by the help of Thy grace, we may be mercifully hastened along when our sins weigh us down" (Collect). Christmas can mean the complete revivifying of the desert of our world. Certainly it can mean the revivifying of the desert of our own souls.

Thus do the words of the Introit take on meaning for us: "Drop down dew, ye heavens, from above, and let the clouds rain down the Just One: let the earth be opened and bud forth a Savior." We are the soil. We may be spiritually dried up, but no soil is beyond repair if it gets enough rain. We need the rain of Christmas grace so that from us the Savior may be born for our world, thus fulfilling the destiny St. Paul pictures for us: "Let a man so account us, as servants of Christ and stewards of the mysteries of God" (Epistle).

GIFT-GIVING

But we must make ourselves ready for Christ by the plowing and harrowing of penance and self-denial. John the Baptist is the master farmer who directs those operations. To us as to his own people he preaches "A baptism of repentance for the forgiveness of sins. Make ready the way of the Lord, make straight his paths. Every valley shall be filled, and every mountain and hill shall be brought low, and the crooked shall be made straight, and the rough ways smooth; and all mankind shall see the salvation of God" (Gospel). We must begin now to prepare our Christmas confession. And we must continue to cultivate the land of our soul by sorrow and repentance throughout the year. If we do this, then surely "all flesh shall see the salvation of God."

The Christmas joy and happiness that we usually associate with giftgiving, Midnight Mass, family gatherings, friendliness and good cheer are as natural as the "happiness" of dry soil after a five-inch rain. Gift-giving and gift-receiving mean love. And it all goes back to God's love for us when at Bethlehem He gave His greatest Gift to us, His Son.

But we must never forget that in Bethlehem there was an exchange of gifts. God's Son took on our humanity, and He in turn gave us His Divinity. That exchange continues, at least, Christ wants it to continue. At Christmas He will again give Himself to us. But we must give ourselves to Him, open our hearts to receive Him so that we in turn can give Him to our world. "Having received Thy gifts, we pray Thee, O Lord, that the frequent reception of this Sacrament may advance the work of our salvation" (Postcommunion prayer).

FOOD FOR THE WAY

1. My mouth shall speak the praise of the Lord: and let all flesh bless His Holy Name. Alleluia, alleluia. Come, O Lord, and do not delay; forgive the sins of Thy people (Gradual and alleluia verses).
2. Hail, Mary, full of grace, the Lord is with Thee. Blessed art thou among women and blessed is the fruit of thy womb (Offertory verse)!
3. Make ready the way of the Lord, make straight his paths (Gospel)!

CHRISTMAS

LIGHT OF MEN

"Come, Lord Jesus... Teach us Thy ways... Enlighten the darkness of our minds by the grace of Thy visitation." Such has been our prayer these last few weeks. That prayer is answered tonight: "Do not be afraid, for behold, I bring you good news of great joy which shall be to all the people; for there has been born to you today in the town of David a Savior, who is Christ the Lord" (Gospel, Midnight Mass).

Who is this Savior? God Himself tells us: He is His own Son. "With Thee is the principality in the day of Thy strength; in the brightness of the saints, from the womb the day-star I begot Thee... Thou art My Son, this day have I begotten Thee (Gradual and Alleluia verses). The Savior of men, the Child of the manger, the Son of Mary the Virgin, is the great high God, equal in all things to the Father. But He is also God's Goodness and Kindness appearing to men (Epistle, 2nd Mass), the One who manifests to us the light of His Father's glory (Preface). He is the Life that is the Light of men (Gospel, 3rd Mass). He is PEACE ON EARTH to all who receive Him. He is EMMANUEL, God-with-us.

24

MAY WE BE FOUND LIKE TO HIM

Why is the Son of God made flesh? "As many as received Him, He gave them power *to be made the sons of God*" (Gospel, 3rd Mass). God becomes man in order to save men from hell and to give them the great joy of sharing His Life. "O Wondrous exchange: the Creator of the human race, taking unto Himself a living body, deigns to be born of a Virgin: and becoming man from no human generation, *hath bestowed upon us His divinity*" (Vesper antiphon, Feast of the Circumcision). He made His Life, His Divinity, available to us by His birth, life, death, resurrection. We receive It in holy Baptism.

What then, we may wonder, is the meaning of this year's Nativity? The Postcommunion of the Midnight Mass prays "that we who rejoice in celebrating the birth of our Lord Jesus Christ, may deserve *by worthy conduct to be admitted into His company.*" We are one with Christ through Baptism. He lives in us, but not fully. His will is still far from being our will. And therefore we pray that we may daily and yearly learn to let Christ live in us, to give in to His way of thinking and doing, so that at the end of this world's living, the Father may say to us: You are my sons; enter into this day of eternity. "Grant that through this holy interchange of gifts, *we may be found like unto Him*, who has united our human nature with the Divine" (Secret, Midnight Mass).

And so we re-emphasize what has already often been indicated: Advent, Christmas, and the whole

Church Year have this important purpose — to help us ultimately to enjoy His happiness in heaven, the mystery of Whose light we have known on earth (Collect, Midnight Mass). From the intensified union with Christ that this Feast provides comes peace of soul now which is a pledge and a foretaste of final peace in eternity. It is very important to remember this idea and to have confidence in it in these days. One of the great graces of Christmas is to help us see in the darkness of the world-wide chaos God's eternal desire and will to save us forever, not just for a few years of security here.

CHRISTMAS AND APOSTOLATE

However, we must beware lest our Christmas celebration, with its glimpses into eternity, make us lose sight of the work Christ expects us to do for Him in our lifetime. Christmas re-enacts our Lord's birth. He becomes one of us so that we may become one with Him, but also that *our world may become one with Him*. His birth means good tidings of great joy for *all the* people. This Feast means, then, the encyclicals of Pius XI on the social question and the lay apostolate. It means Pius XII's encyclicals on the Mystical Body and Liturgy. It means social justice, racial justice, tolerance, charity.

It is a call to all of us to contemplate the goodness and kindness of God in His gift of Himself to us and then to carry the fruits of our contemplation into our environment so that it may become Christ's. This implies the individual dedication of each of us to furthering the ideals of Christ as given to us by His Vicars. It means patience and kindness in our homes, forgiveness of enemies, consideration for the human weakness of our brethren, active charity, and a never-ending effort to promote unity in our parishes and communities.

We spoke above about peace of soul. But this might well be a luxury in these modern times. It might well be that peace of soul is the reward Christ gives us only after we have spent ourselves in promoting His cause. Perhaps the greatest grace we could receive from this wonderful celebration would be to see Christ and Christmas as the Way and the Light given into our hands so that we might help Him to dispel the darkness of despair in our world and thus make it easier for our fellow men to be saved forever.

REJOICE

But nothing should curtail our rejoicing in this great event. We are members of the Church, Christ's Mystical Body. And the Church is ever a rejoicing Church because she knows that "The Lord hath made known His salvation" (Gradual, 3rd Mass) and that "With the Lord there is mercy, and with Him plentiful redemption" (Vespers Antiphon). "Let the heavens rejoice, and let the earth be glad before the face of the Lord, because He cometh" (Offertory verse, Midnight Mass).

But as the Church exhorts us to rejoice, she also urges us to remember our blessed condition as redeemed: "Remember, O Christian, thy dignity: thou hast been made a partaker of the divine nature. Do not return to thy former base way of life" (St. Leo, Matins

Lesson). And she tells us plainly of a program of life that will not only bring peace of soul to us now and at the end, but also a more fruitful apostolate in our efforts to bring "plentiful redemption" to our world: "Rejecting ungodliness and worldly lusts, live temperately and justly and piously in this world; looking for the blessed hope and glorious coming of our great God and Savior, Jesus Christ" (Epistle, Midnight Mass). The power to carry out that program is not wanting to us. All we have to do is to pray: "May the new life derived from this Sacrament *ever revive us*, O Lord: since it is His Sacrament, whose wonderful birth hath overcome the old man" (Postcommunion, 2nd Mass).

FOOD FOR THE WAY

1. Glory to God in the highest, and peace on earth to men of good will (Gospel, Midnight Mass).
2. Holy, Holy, Holy, Lord God of Hosts, the heavens and the earth are full of Thy glory. Hosanna in the highest. Blessed is He that cometh in the Name of the Lord (Preface).
3. But Mary kept in mind all these words, pondering them in her heart (Gospel, 2nd Mass).

FEAST OF ST. STEPHEN, DECEMBER 26

FULL OF GRACE AND FORTITUDE

St. Stephen is called the Church's first martyr. He was the first of Christ's followers to give witness to Christ by His death. It is therefore fitting that the Church should celebrate his feast day, his nativity into eternal glory, immediately after the nativity of the God he served so briefly but so perfectly.

The story of Stephen's apostolate is given in the Epistle of this Mass. We are told first of all what kind of man he was: "Full of grace and fortitude — full of faith and the Holy Spirit." There is no need for us to wonder about the source of his inner life and strength. He was so united with Christ that "looking up steadfastly to heaven, he saw the glory of God and Jesus standing at the right hand of God."

This union with Christ and its results in his life made his apostolate irresistible. He did great wonders and signs among the people, and his enemies were not able to resist the wisdom and spirit that spoke through him. Their hearts being surrounded by the steel of worldliness, they took the only course open to them... or what they thought was the only course. They stoned him, "and the witnesses laid down their garments at the feet of a young man, whose name was Saul." But Stephen was the perfect disciple of Christ to the very end. As he lay dying, he prayed for his killers: "Lord, lay not this sin to their charge. And when he had said this, he fell asleep in the Lord." Father, forgive them, they know not what they do.

The Church isolates several facts from this epistle and uses them with special emphasis for our sake in other parts of the Mass. These facts are: Stephen's prayer for his enemies; his being filled with faith and the Holy Spirit; and his seeing the heavens opened and Jesus standing at the right hand of God. The connection between these facts is very close.

STEPHEN AND WE

It requires no imagination to deduce from these facts and from the feast itself that St. Stephen was and is a perfect model for all lay apostles. If we would have our apostolate bear fruit, we too must be full of faith and the Holy Spirit as he was. We can receive that faith and that Holy Spirit by constantly and steadfastly looking up to heaven in mental prayer and by living with Christ in His liturgical year. This close contact with God will give us the correct attitude towards men. Being filled with love for God and desire for His glory, we will see them all — even our enemies and those who want nothing to do with Christ — as potential sharers with us of the vision of the glory of God, and we will be impelled to bring them to God Who is so deserving of more and more love. We will love them and pray for them, even while they "stone" us.

Our results may not be great. Stephen was cut off from his apostolate in high youth. We never know what fruit our efforts will bring, just as Stephen hardly knew that the young man named Saul would one day far out-do him in bringing men to Christ. (Some Church Fathers think that Stephen's martyrdom won for Saul the grace of conversion). At any rate, the blood of martyrs is the seed of Christians, a truth that holds in any age of the Church. The youth named Saul, who stood by enjoying the shedding of Stephen's blood, became Paul *the* Apostle who wonderfully completed what Stephen had begun. "May the mysteries which we receive help us, O Lord : and through the intercession of Blessed Stephen Thy Martyr, may they strengthen us with thine ever-lasting protection" (Postcommunion prayer) and with the fullness of fortitude and the Holy Spirit for our apostolate !

FOOD FOR THE WAY

1. Blessed are the undefiled in the way, who walk in the law of the Lord (Introit).
2. Behold I see the heavens opened, and the Son of Man standing on the right hand of God (Epistle)!
3. Jerusalem, Jerusalem, thou that killest the prophets, and stonest them that are sent unto thee, how often would I have gathered together thy children, as the hen doth gather her chickens under her wings, and thou wouldst not (Gospel)?

31

ST. JOHN THE APOSTLE,
DECEMBER 27

THE DISCIPLE JESUS LOVED

Second place in honor after our Lord's birth goes to "the disciple whom Jesus loved, the one who, at the supper, had leaned back on his breast and said 'Lord, who is it that will betray Thee' " (Gospel)? Christ loved all His apostles. They were His friends. They had left all things to follow Him. But St. John is singled out as the one whom Jesus seemed to love more than the rest. It is not hard to figure out why.

He was known as the virgin apostle, the one whose love had belonged only to God. The Epistle tells how God rewarded him: "If a man fears the Lord, he will live an upright life. If a man holds fast to innocence, he will find her in his embrace, welcoming him as a mother welcomes the son who cherishes her. Long life and good discernment are the bread this mother will provide for him, wisdom the reviving draught she will give him to drink... The Lord our God has joy and triumph in store for him, and will enrich him with a name that shall never be forgotten" (Knox translation).

St. John found his joy and triumph in following Christ. On the mount of the Transfiguration He saw his Master transfigured and heard the Father say : "This is My beloved Son, in whom I am well pleased." At the Last Supper he leaned on Jesus's breast and recorded the magnificent last discourse of Christ (Chapters 13 to 18 of his Gospel). He followed Him to the Garden of Olives where he saw Him sweat blood and heard Him say: "Not my will but Thine be done." The others fled, but John remained and stood beneath the cross with Mary. He heard Jesus give Mary to him as his Mother, and he took her to himself. Christ rose from the dead and dwelt with them for forty days. Now it is time for Him to ascend to heaven. "Peter therefore, seeing John, said to Jesus, 'Lord, what of this man?' Jesus said to him, 'If I wish him to remain until I come, what is it to thee? Do you follow me?' This saying therefore went abroad among the brethren, that that disciple was not to die. But Jesus had not said to him, 'He is not to die'; but rather, 'If I wish him to remain until I come, what is it to thee' " (Gospel)?

GOD IS LOVE

It would almost seem that it was our Lord's will that John should remain on earth longer than the others so that we might have the benefit of all that he had learned by leaning on His Sacred Heart and which he was to give forth to the world in the form of his Gospel and his Epistles of love; and above all that we might have the benefit of his example of closeness to Christ. "The innocent man will flourish as the palm tree flourishes ; he will grow to greatness as the cedars grow on Lebanon" (Offertory verse, Knox translation).

St. John probably never had as many converts as the other apostles. But the millions of his readers who have fed on the fruit of his vision of God have made of him a flourishing tree of everbearing fruit. "In the midst of the Church he opened his mouth; and the Lord filled him with the spirit of wisdom and understanding; He clothed him with a robe of glory" (Introit).

John tells us the essential things that we need for our life, for our apostolate: "God is love. In this has the love of God been shown in our case, that God has sent His only begotten Son into the world that we may live through him... God is love, and he who abides in love abides in God, and God in him" (1 John 4:9-16). God is love... this was the final outcome of all his years of study and prayer. If we too can come to realize that God is love, and if we abide in that love, He will live in us, and our apostolate will bear fruit. The test of our love for God is our love for our neighbor and our untiring efforts to bring others to know that love as we know it.

At the end of his life St. John preached only one sermon. Every time he was carried to church, he would say: "My little children, love one another." At last his disciples, wearied with his constant refrain, asked him: "Master, why dost thou say this always?" Whereto he replied to them: "It is the commandment of the Lord, and if this is done, it is enough." (Breviary lesson, 2nd Nocturne of the Feast).

In the light of God's love for us as shown in our recent Christmas celebration, we know that John spoke the truth... a most necessary truth for us, for our family, parish, community and school life. And necessary above all in the apostolate where clashes of opinion are even more possible among us than among John's own companions. Love for one another is Christ's own commandment. Christ willed that John should remain to tell us by word and example that there is no true love for God without it.

FOOD FOR THE WAY

1. It is good to give praise to the Lord; and to sing to Thy Name, O Most High (Introit).
2. Do thou follow me (Gospel).
3. In this we have come to know his love, that he laid down his life for us; and we likewise ought to lay down our life for the brethren (1 John 3:16).
4. Little children, love one another.

FEAST OF THE HOLY
INNOCENTS, DECEMBER 28

OUT OF THE MOUTH OF INFANTS

How is the birth of the Son of God received by the world? Practically in silence, except by the little and the humble ones — His mother and foster-father, the shepherds, and the Holy Innocents whose feast we celebrate today. "Out of the mouth of infants, O God, Thou hast perfected praise because of Thine enemies." And what do the Innocents say in praise in the wondrous event of their Savior's birth? "O Lord, our God, how admirable is Thy Name (art Thou and Thy works) in the whole earth" (Introit)!

Of course, the Innocents did not really praise God in that many words. Being only two years old or under (Gospel), they could hardly speak. The Church puts these prophetic words in their mouths. But they did shout their cheers for this beginning of Redemption by *deed*, by sacrifice, by giving up their lives — what there was of them — and since there is always a return from God for every sacrifice, they received waving palms and jeweled crowns, symbolic of eternal joy and happiness.

Prudentius, author of the Vespers hymn, paints the charming picture of these little ones playing with their palms and crowns at the foot of the heavenly altar.

This joyful picture continues in the Epistle, although the imageful language of St. John makes the Innocents, the "first-fruits unto God," a little more reserved. They have been purchased from the earth; they are virgins, i.e. undefiled by sinful contact with the wickedness of the world. "In their mouth there was found no lie; they are without blemish before the throne of God." Their task forever is "to sing as it were a new song before the throne... and to follow the Lamb wherever he goes."

The Gradual shows our young heroes speaking from the heights of heaven, describing in poetic language the martyrdom they suffered for Christ. As a bird escapes the snares of the fowlers, they were delivered from Herod's clutches and from longer life in the harsh world. They lost their life in this world, but they won eternal life with God. And thus they were the first to fulfill Christ's word: "He who would save his life will lose it; but he who loses his life for my sake shall find it. For what does it profit a man, if he gain the whole world, but suffer the loss of his own soul" (Matthew 16:25-26)? "Our help is in the Name of the Lord. Who made heaven and earth. Praise the Lord, ye children, praise ye the Name of the Lord" (Alleluia verse).

The joyful picture thus far in the Mass takes the edge off the cruelty of the actual martyrdom as it is realistically related by St. Matthew in the Gospel. "Herod sent and slew all the boys in Bethlehem who were two years old or under... Then was fulfilled what was spoken through Jeremias the prophet, saying, 'A voice was heard in Rama, weeping and loud lamentation; Rachel weeping for her children, and she would not be comforted, because they are no more." The Jewish mothers' grief is understandable; for they could hardly know that their sons would be saints through whose prayers all future ages would gain help both "in this life and in the life to come" (Postcommunion prayer). The lay apostle needs courage and vision every day of his life — but especially when he sees "innocents" suffer and when he meets with opposition. Courage and vision are available to him through the intercession of the Holy Innocents.

DESTROY EVIL IN US

But we may ask what there is in this Feast for us who are not so innocent. We can find out by examining the Collect. There are three ways of praising God and thus living according to our nature as reasoning, redeemed beings; by word, by deed, and by word and deed together. The Innocents did it by deed, "Not by speaking, but by dying" (Collect). The Church wants us her members to praise God by word and deed together, by sacrifice, by giving up vice and sin, by giving ourselves wholly into God's hands. "Destroy within us the evil of all vice, so that our lives may declare by our deeds Thy faith which our tongues profess" (Collect).

Our martyrdom is to take place in our world, in fidelity to our particular vocations, in carrying a life-long cross after the manner of our Savior, Christ. The result will be the same for us as it was for the Holy Innocents, namely, palms, crowns, harps, HAPPINESS everlasting.

FOOD FOR THE WAY

1. O Lord our God, how admirable is Thy Name in the whole earth (Introit)!
2. Praise the Lord, ye children, praise ye the Name of the Lord (Alleluia verse)!
3. Our soul hath been delivered as a sparrow out of the snare of the fowlers; The snare is broken, and we are delivered (Offertory verse).

SUNDAY BETWEEN
CHRISTMAS AND NEW YEAR'S

MORE THAN MORTAL BEAUTY

This Sunday is a little Christmas. It tenderly reviews the events of that night of nights: "While all things were in quiet silence, and the night was in the midst of her course, Thy almighty Word, O Lord, leapt down from heaven, from Thy royal throne" (Introit). And it describes the Child as only the Holy Spirit, Who best knew Him, could. "Thou are beautiful above the sons of men: grace is poured abroad in Thy lips" (Gradual). The Child at Mary's breast is human, but He is also God: "Thy throne, O God, is prepared from of old; Thou art from everlasting" (Offertory verse). The Word, second Person of the Blessed Trinity, was made flesh and dwells among us (Versicle of 2nd Vespers).

But the Mass also looks into the future of this Child King. He becomes a slave, "even though he is the master of all" (Epistle). With Joseph and Mary, His Mother, we may well marvel at the things spoken concerning Him. Nevertheless, this child is destined for the fall and the rise of many in Israel, and for a sign that

shall be contradicted" (Gospel). The eternal throne is
going to become an earthly one: it will be from a sign
of contradiction, a cross, that He will reign, drawing
men to Himself, and eventually from an altar of sacrifice.
The fullness of time has come, and God has "sent His
Son, born of a woman, born under the law, *that he
might redeem* those who were under the law, that we
might *receive the adoption of sons.*" For this was the
Son of God born — that through Him men might be
released from their condition as slaves of Satan and hell
and restored to full membership as *sons* in the family of
the Heavenly Father, sharers in His love and life and
heirs of His eternal joys and glory.

A SWORD IN THY SOUL

"And because you are sons, God has sent the Spirit
of His Son into your hearts, crying, 'Abba, Father.' So
that he is no longer a slave, but a son; and if a son, an
heir also through God" (Epistle). But before we can
come into the fullness of our inheritance as God's sons,
the words of old Simon must be fulfilled in all of us, as
they were in Mary: "Thy own soul a sword shall pierce,
that the thoughts of many hearts may be revealed"
(Gospel).

And so, even in the midst of Christmas joy, we are
reminded of the Passion and Death of the Savior, and
of the necessity of our sharing in His complete life, dark
days as well as joyous. We do not know the kind of
sword that will pierce our hearts, nor the depth it will

reach. Certainly none of us will be tried as fiercely as Mary, Mother of Sorrows.

But if we are tried, we have Christ in us to uphold us. Mary, Simeon, and the prophetess Anna held Him in their arms. We have Him as our Food. He becomes for us the grace of tender devotion and the reward of a happy eternity (Secret prayer). But most of all He acts in us, purging out our vices and satisfying our just desires (Postcommunion prayer).

If we take this Child and His Mother and go into our life in the world, keeping them always for our inspiration and our light, then we too shall grow and become strong and become full of wisdom. And the grace of God will be upon us (Gospel).

FOOD FOR THE WAY

1. The Lord hath reigned, He is clothed with beauty: the Lord is clothed with strength, and hath girded Himself (Introit).
2. Joyful the thoughts that well up from my heart, a King's honour for my theme: my tongue flows readily as the pen of a swift writer (Gradual, Knox translation).
3. God hath established the world, which shall not be moved: Thy throne, O God, is prepared from of old; Thou art from everlasting (Offertory verse).

FEAST OF THE CIRCUMCISION
and OCTAVE OF CHRISTMAS

A RIGHT BEGINNING

The Octave of Christmas and the Feast of our Lord's Circumcision is a holy day of obligation. With her sense of values, the Church knows that, like it or not, her children should begin the new year with benefit of the central Sacrifice whence flows all grace, light, and help into their lives. And besides, Christmas deserves all the celebration they can give it. "Sing joyfully to God, all the earth. The Lord hath made known His salvation" (Gradual).

Eight days have passed since the night of the angels' song of glory to God. Eight nights ago we were all aglow with expectation and tenderness. On Christmas we heard the Church say to us: "A Child is born to us, and a Son is given to us: Whose government is upon His shoulder: and His name shall be called the Angel of great counsel. Sing ye to the Lord a new canticle: because He hath done wonderful things." We hear that very same Introit today; and if we do not thrill to it now as we did then, it could be that there is more sentimentality than true, sacrificial love for our Lord in our religion.

And that is all the more reason for sinking our teeth into the Epistle, a repeat from the first Mass of Christmas. "The grace of God our Saviour has appeared to all men, instructing us, that, rejecting ungodliness and worldly lusts, we may live temperately and justly and piously in this world; looking for the blessed hope and glorious coming of our great God and Savior, Jesus Christ, *who gave himself for us that he might redeem us from all iniquity* and cleanse for himself an acceptable people, pursuing good works." The whole life of Jesus and the purpose of His coming and what we should do about it is there summed up. He gave Himself for us... that He might redeem us from *all* iniquity. What we must do is negatively to reject ungodliness and worldly lusts, and positively to live temperately and justly and piously in this world (which means living always in His presence and seeing life through His eyes). It would be interesting to contrast our New Year's Eve activity with that program.

CIRCUMCISING HEARTS

Today we can see that Jesus took His share in the redemptive work seriously. The Gospel tells how He submitted to the Jewish law of the Circumcision and thus shed the first drops of His precious blood. Thus the life long sacrifice of Himself for us begins. Calvary and the full out-pouring of that blood appear in the near future. Whenever we hear of our Lord's blood poured out in sacrifice, we must think of our sins that caused the flow of that blood. Christ redeemed us; but we have to stay redeemed *by a continual circumcision of these sin-inclined hearts of ours* lest His blood be shed in vain. That is why both the Secret and Postcommunion prayers of this Mass speak about "cleansing us," and "washing away our guilt."

Most of us have to learn the hard way that the negative rejecting of ungodliness and worldly lusts can hardly be successful without God's help, and specifically without the Eucharist and the intercession of Mary. The Postcommunion is therefore a good prayer for the whole year: "May this Communion, O Lord, wash away our guilt and make us ready, through the intercession of the Blessed Virgin Mary, Mother of God, to share in this heavenly remedy."

Mary is very prominent in this Feast. Both Collect and Postcommunion are prayed through her intercession, and most of the antiphons of Vespers celebrate her "fruitful virginity." "In the bush which Moses saw was not burnt, we acknowledge the figure of thy glorious inviolate virginity: Mother of God, intercede for us" (Third antiphon of Vespers). By her consent to God's will she became mother of the Savior and mother of us all. We can sing a new canticle to the Lord today and always because He has done wonderful things in giving us so generous a Savior and so loving a Mother.

FOOD FOR THE WAY

1. Thine are the heavens and Thine is the earth: the world and the fulness thereof Thou hast founded;

justice and judgment are the preparation of Thy throne. (Offertory verse).

2. God, who diversely spoke in times past to the fathers by the prophets, last of all in these days hath spoken to us by His son. Alleluia. (Alleluia verse).

3. Sing ye to the Lord a new canticle: because He hath done wonderful things (Introit).

SUNDAY BETWEEN THE CIRCUMCISION and EPIPHANY

JESUS

From the beginning of the history of salvation, God gave people names which summed up the nature, the character and the work they were to do. His own Son was no exception to this rule. "At that time, when eight days were fulfilled for the circumcision of the child, his name was called Jesus, the name given him by the angel before he was conceived in the womb" (Gospel). St. Matthew relates how the angel of the Lord appeared to Joseph and informed him of Mary's condition. "That which is begotten in her is of the Holy Spirit. And she shall bring forth a son, and thou shalt call his name Jesus ; for he shall save his people from their sins (Matthew 1:21). The name Jesus, therefore, means Savior, and that is why it is so precious to us.

This Mass gives us a beautiful picture of the respect and admiration that Holy Name commands and of the power it possesses if rightly used. In the Introit we see the vision of every knee in heaven, on earth and under the earth bending in awe at the very mention of the

47

name Jesus. Which is as it should be, for Jesus is God as well as man. "O Lord, our Lord, how wonderful is Thy Name in the whole earth" (Introit)!

The power inherent in Jesus' name rightly invoked is set forth in the Epistle. Peter had cured a cripple simply by saying to him: "In the Name of Jesus Christ of Nazareth, arise and walk" (Acts 3:6). He was brought to trial and this was his defense: "If we are on trial today about a good work done to a cripple... be it known to all of you and to all the people of Israel that *in the name of our Lord Jesus Christ* of Nazareth, whom you crucified, whom God has raised from the dead, even in this name does he stand here before you, sound... There is no other name under heaven given to men by which we must be saved" (Epistle). Angels, saints, poor souls, and even the damned in hell bend their knee at the very sound of the name of Jesus. His name invoked on a cripple makes the sick man whole. But in our land, for a great many men, and even women and children, that blessed Name is little more than a convenient exclamation used to emphasize a boastful opinion.

THE NAME CHRISTIAN

We too have a name, with a special meaning. We are called *Christians*, a name that expresses better than any other our nature, our character, and our work. Our name means that we are redeemed, that we are followers of Christ, His brothers, and that we are his apostolic representatives in our world. Christ acted according to His inner nature in saving us by dying for us. We can act according to our nature, indicated by our name, by becoming more and more redeemed, and by our apostolic work. "Save us, O Lord, our God, and gather us from among the nations: that we may give thanks to Thy Holy Name, and may glory in Thy praise. Thou, O Lord, are our Father and Redeemer" (Gradual). Such is the prayer of our world. It is within our power to bring about a happy answer to that prayer. Hallowed be Thy Name... Thy Kingdom come... Thy will be done!

But our apostolate will be fruitful in proportion to our hold on the Name of Jesus, our being more and more redeemed, more and more one with Him. We become more and more one with Him by engraving the name and doctrine of Jesus ("Not my will, but Thine be done") more and more deeply into our conscious daily life. And above all, by filling our souls with the fruit of Christ's redeeming work, Divine Life, which fruit we can pick from its ever-abundant source, Holy Mass.

"Jesu, the very thought of Thee with sweetness fills
    my breast,
But sweeter far Thy face to see, and in Thy presence
    rest.
Nor voice can sing, nor heart can frame, nor can the
    memory find,
A sweeter sound than Thy blest Name, O Savior of
    mankind" (Vespers hymn)!

1. O Lord, our Lord, how wonderful is Thy Name in the whole earth (Introit)!

2. My mouth shall speak the praise of the Lord, and let all flesh bless His Holy Name (Alleluia verse)!

3. I will praise Thee, O Lord, my God, with my whole heart, and I will glorify Thy Name forever; for Thou, O Lord, are sweet and mild, and plenteous in mercy to all that call upon Thee. Alleluia (Offertory verse).

EPIPHANY

BEHOLD THE LORD THE RULER

"Behold the Lord the Ruler is come: and a kingdom is in His hand, and power and dominion" (Introit). The Epiphany is one of the greatest of our Lord's feasts. In the eyes of the Church it has a higher rank even than Christmas ; and in Europe, Canada, and Mexico it is a holy day of obligation. At first glance, Epiphany is not so emotionally attractive to us as Christmas is — a King seated on a majestic throne hardly appeals to human eyes as strongly as does a new-born child — but a profound grasp of the spirit of the texts of this Feast will reveal it to us eventually as tremendously beautiful and alluring.

The Magnificat antiphon of 2nd Vespers give the contents of the feast: "We keep this day holy in honor of three miracles: this day a star led the Wise Men to the manger; this day water was turned into wine at the marriage feast; this day Christ chose to be baptized by John in the Jordan, for our salvation. Alleluia." What is common to all three of these miracles is the *manifestation of Jesus' divinity*. All three manifestations are included in our celebration now, but today the Church emphasizes the manifestation to the Magi, leaving the other two "epiphanies" to the Octave day and the second Sunday to follow.

The Gospel shows us the plain picture of the Magi, led miraculously by a star, coming to the child with all their royal retinue. Without asking themselves how a little child could be King and Savior, they immediately fall down and worship Him. And, as symbols of their gift of self to Him, they open their treasures and offer Him gold, frankincense, and myrrh.

Such is the quiet simple scene. But it was this that the Prophet Isaias had foretold hundreds of years before: "Arise, be enlightened, O Jerusalem, for thy light has come, and the glory of the Lord has arisen upon thee. For behold darkness covers the earth, and a mist the peoples; but the Lord rises as a light upon thee, and his glory is seen upon thee. And the Gentiles shall walk in thy light, and the kings in the brightness of thy rising... the possessions of the Gentiles shall come to thee... all they from Saba shall come, bringing gold and frankincense, and proclaiming the praise of the Lord" (Epistle). He who is Lord of heaven and earth enters into His earthly kingdom to take possession of it. "Behold the Lord the Ruler is come: and a kingdom is in His hand, and power and dominion."

THE BEAUTY OF HIS MAJESTY

But one of the Magi offered myrrh to Him. Jesus is King. But He is to come into His kingdom by His death. The myrrh was symbolic of His burial. But He will rise from death and will enlighten and feed His subjects and will Himself be their sacrifice. "Graciously regard the gifts of Thy Church: in which gold, frankincense and myrrh are no longer laid before Thee; but He is sacrificed and received who by these very gifts was signified, Jesus Christ Thy Son our Lord" (Secret prayer). He is working now to fill up His Kingdom. When that kingdom is filled, He will come again as King of Glory in the final Epiphany, of which this is but the preview.

We in the apostolate are helping to prepare and to bring on that great Epiphany, that last decisive coming and manifestation of our King. Then we shall know the glorious result of our work. We know and serve Him now by faith, but this service will inevitably lead us to "gaze on the beauty of His majesty" (Collect).

THEY ADORED HIM

This feast is for our world, covered with the darkness and mist of a God-denying way of life. To our world the King Christ says: "I am your Way, your Truth, your Life." He says that from the throne of His Mother's arms, from the throne of the altar at this and every Mass, and He will say it from His throne of Judgment at the end of time. If our world, like Herod, shows only minor interest in Him, or is disturbed at His kingdom, or says it will come and adore but does not mean it, it will suffer the fate of Herod. "Those who sought the Child's life are dead" (Matthew 2:20).

Drawn by the great Light Isaias saw, we approach our churches today, bearing in our hearts our most precious gifts. We offer the *myrrh* of our death to sin, and we offer the pure *gold* of our love which will make us resolve to direct our lives to God even as *incense* rising up fragrantly as from a fiery coal.

When we hear these words of the gospel, "Falling down they adored Him," we must let our imitation of the Magis' genuflection really express our entire gift of ourselves to Christ our King, and through Him to the Father. If we do this in the light of the texts of this Mass, a great light will rise in our souls, showing us Him who is our true King, the acceptance of whom will eventually lead to the contemplation of the eternal Beauty of God's Majesty. Holy Mass is not obligatory today under pain of mortal sin, but it is under pain of missing our Lord's desire to show Himself to us.

FOOD FOR THE WAY

1. We have seen His star in the east: and have come with gifts to adore the Lord (Alleluia verse).
2. All the kings of the earth shall adore Him; all nations shall serve Him (Offertory verse).
3. It is truly fit and just... always and in all places, to give thanks unto Thee, O Holy Lord, Father Almighty, Eternal God; because Thine only-begotten Son has manifested Himself in the substance of our mortal nature. (Preface).

FEAST OF THE HOLY FAMILY

HOUSE OF THE LORD

"That all may be one, even as thou, Father, in me and I in thee; that they may be one in us, that the world may believe that thou hast sent me" (John 17:21). When at the end of His life, our Lord prayed that prayer, He was thinking of His Mystical Body, His Church: His Church such as it was gathered together around Him there in the Upper Room, His Church such as it would be in future ages throughout the world. He was also thinking of the units that would go to make up that Church — the parishes and the cells that would compose the parishes, the families. Some 1900 years after our Lord's prayer for unity, His representative on earth, Leo XIII instituted the Feast of the Holy Family as at least a partial answer to that prayer. The full answer will come when Christian families all over the world will base their life together on the ideals and principles of this Feast.

The Feast first of all presents the attractive portrait of the perfect family, Jesus, Mary, and Joseph, and tells us: "This is what your family life should be." The one thing that makes it perfect is that *God is in its midst* in the person of Jesus. "Truly Thou art a hidden King, the God of Israel, the Savior" (Alleluia verse). And the will of the Father is the will of all its members. The parents love their Son as no other child could ever be loved; but God has given Him to them, so they in turn "take Him up to Jerusalem to present Him to the Lord" (Offertory verse). The Son for His part loves His mother and foster-father to a degree that only His Father in heaven is loved more. "He was subject to them" (Gospel).

This Holy Family did everything together: they worked, they rested, and above all they prayed *together*. Together they went up to the House of the Lord in Jerusalem singing as they went along the way: "How lovely are Thy tabernacles, O Lord of hosts; my soul longeth and fainteth for the courts of the Lord" (Introit). We can be certain that they did not leave their praying and singing in the temple. Simeon had prophesied: "This child is destined for the fall and for the rise of many in Israel, and for a sign that shall be contradicted. And thy own soul a sword shall pierce." They belong to God. His will is their will. Therefore there is no anxiety, no worry about the future. Calvary will come, but Easter will follow just as inevitably. The Father of the Just One rejoices greatly. His father and mother are joyful; and she who bore Him rejoices exceedingly (Introit).

THE BOND OF PERFECTION

"O Lord Jesus Christ, Who didst consecrate family life with sublime virtues, in Thy obedience to Mary and

Joseph ; by their help, grant that we may be instructed in this example of Thy Holy Family and thus obtain a share in their eternal happiness" (Collect).

The way before us, in our family and parish life, is plain. To do our part in helping to fulfill Christ's prayer for unity, we must strive to make our families and parishes holy. (If we start with the cell of the parish organism, the family, the unity and health of the parish itself will certainly follow). The Christian family should be one in mind, in spirit, and in will, not only because its members are united by bonds of blood, but above all because they are united in Christ. Christ is in them. The same divine Life that is in Christ is in them all; and they are closer to one another by the bond of the Christ-life than they are by bonds of blood. Whatever they do to one another, they do to Christ.

The family members therefore will have a passion for unity and togetherness, and they will abhor any selfish individualism that threatens to destroy their togetherness. They will work, play, live, and eat together. They will know that keeping their unity and reducing selfishness, the great destroyer, will be impossible without prayer and sacrifice together both in the home and in the parish church. They will frequently read the story of salvation in the Gospels, feeding on the word of God and learning from God Himself His eternal desire for unity among men. They will know that in the official prayer of the Church, Prime and Compline, as well as their parish community Mass, they have the very same prayer that Christ Himself used in His earthly days. A more fruitful source of unity could not be found. For in the Mass Christ Himself pleads for them, as is so wonderfully shown in today's Secret prayer: "We offer Thee, O Lord, this Victim of our ransom, and by the intercession of the God-bearing Virgin, together with blessed Joseph, we fervently implore Thee firmly to establish our families in Thy peace and grace."

But St. Paul says all this in inspired words that ought to be engraved in the hearts of all parents and children: "Brethren: put on, as God's chosen ones, holy and beloved, a heart of mercy, kindness, humility, meekness, patience. Bear with one another and forgive one another, if anyone has a grievance against any other... But above all these things have charity, which is the bond of perfection. And may the peace of Christ reign in your hearts... Show yourselves thankful. Let the word of Christ dwell in you abundantly: in all wisdom teach and admonish one another by psalms, hymns and spiritual songs, singing in your hearts to God... Whatever you do, do all in the name of the Lord Jesus Christ, giving thanks to God the Father" (Epistle).

TRUE REALISM

All this may sound unrealistic to modern Catholic families, but that is only because so few of them really try it. Those who have done all in their power to found truly Christian families after the model of Nazareth find that family life together is already now a foretaste of life in their eternal home and that their house is even now a "House of the Lord." "One thing I have asked of the Lord: this will I seek after: that I may dwell in the house of the Lord all the days of my life" (Gradual).

They also find that interest in the unity of their parish increases. For love and union cannot be exclusive: they necessarily turn outward in a strong demand to be shared in by others. A parish composed of this kind of holy families necessarily attracts those who are not of the fold. This is the old apostolic device of the early Christians. The pagans saw how the Christians loved one another, how they worked and prayed together, and they were irresistibly drawn to enter into communities to share that love and union. That can happen today.

FOOD FOR THE WAY

1. How lovely are Thy tabernacles, O Lord of hosts; my soul longeth and fainteth for the courts of the Lord (Introit)!

2. Blessed are they who dwell in Thy house, O Lord; they shall praise Thee forever and ever (Gradual).

3. Jesus went down with them, and came to Nazareth and was subject to them (Communion verse).

SUNDAY WITHIN OCTAVE
OF EPIPHANY

ONE BODY IN CHRIST

The Mass of the Sunday within the Octave of Epiphany is replaced by that of the Holy Family and therefore has to be celebrated on Monday. It is unfortunate that most of the people cannot share in this Mass, since it is as beautiful and instructive as any in the whole Church Year. Moreover, it retains more of the Epiphany spirit of joyful mystery than the Holy Family Mass, although it does resemble the latter Mass very much.

The Epiphany theme is to be found in the Introit, the Gradual and Alleluia verse, and the Offertory. "Upon a high throne I saw a Man sitting, Whom a multitude of angels adore singing together: Behold Him the name of Whose empire is forever" (Introit). "Blessed be the Lord, the God of Israel, Who alone doth wonderful things from the beginning" (Gradual). "Sing joyfully to God all the earth, serve ye the Lord with gladness: come in before His presence with exceeding great joy: *for the Lord He is God*" (Offertory verse).

The Gospel is the same as that of the Holy Family Mass; and the Epistle gives a clear picture of the Family of God, the Mystical Body of Christ, of which every Christian family is a living cell: "For as in one body we have many members, but all the members have not the same office; so we, being many, are *one body in Christ, and every one members one of another.*"

The Family of God, of which Christ is the head and we the members, is the model of every Christian family. Or, as Father Parsch points out, the Christian family is a small edition of the Mystical Body. One of the best ways of coming to a realization of the true nature and functioning of the Mystical Body is to understand marriage and family life. In the Christian family the father takes the place of Christ. The mother represents the Church. The children are the members of the body. Each has his own work to do... "all the members have not the same office" (Epistle), but whatever the work, it is necessary for the well-being of the whole. The father needs the wife and is incomplete without her, and so also does the wife need the husband. They are one: one mind, one body, one will, one purpose. The more husband and wife love one another, the more their union will be blessed in their children. (So also do we need the Savior and the Savior needs us, as Pius XII points out in his encyclical *Mystici Corporis*, Par. 44; "It is manifestly clear that the faithful need the help of the divine Redeemer... Yet this, too, must be held, marvelous though it appear: *Christ requires His members).*

To return to our comparison of the human family with the family of God: The father provides food for the family, and the mother distributes it to the children, just as do Christ and the Church, His Spouse. From father and mother the children receive life and inspiration. But here is an important thought: in the true Christian family, just as in the family of God, there is but one thought, one will — the thought and will of God the Father. To make that will of God one's own is the lifework of every person and every collection of persons. It is the only program that can bring peace in our families and in the family of nations.

THE FATHER'S BUSINESS

And the will of God is the burden of this Mass. It begins in the Collect ("God grant that we may both perceive what we ought to do and have strength to accomplish the same"); continues in the Epistle ("Be not conformed to this world, but be reformed in the newness of your mind, that you may prove what is the good, and the acceptable, and *the perfect will of God*"); and it stands out in supreme clarity in the Gospel ("Did you not know that I must be about My Father's business?")

We need never wonder what God's will is for us. Our particular vocation determines that. To do everything well that is required by our vocation (and that includes the little things): to offer ourselves and works (including the little things from a motive of love for Him ; to be ready to accept with total resignation to Him anything that He might send to try us; and to do all in our power to bring about unity in our families, our parishes, our world — all this is to do God's will, to be about His business.

62

FOOD FOR THE WAY

1. O sing joyfully to the Lord, all the earth: serve ye the Lord with gladness (Introit).

2. May the sacrifice which is offered to Thee, O Lord, always quicken and protect us (Secret).

SECOND SUNDAY AFTER EPIPHANY

SHOUT WITH JOY

As we indicated on the Feast of the Epiphany, the Church celebrated three of our Lord's manifestations on that day, the most prominent being the showing forth of His divinity to the Gentiles in the persons of the Magi. The other two are the baptism of Christ in the Jordan (when the Father revealed Him to the multitudes as His Son) and the miracle of the changing of water into wine at the Cana wedding feast (where He manifested His glory to His apostles). It is this latter manifestation that claims our attention today. And here is the way the Church feels about the birth and "epiphanies" of Jesus (it is also the way she wants us to feel):

"Let all the earth adore Thee, O God, and sing to Thee: let it sing a psalm to Thy Name, O Thou Most High. Shout with joy to God, all the earth: give glory to His praise" (Introit)!

It seems that when the Church celebrates, she really lets herself go... like the young Bride that she is. (That is another meaning for the Epiphany: it is the wedding feast between Christ and His Spouse the Church. As the Benedictus antiphon of the Feast has it: "Today the Church is united to her heavenly Bridegroom..."). Therefore, we must see the Church as a Bride in full and glorious union with her Bridegroom if we would understand her great joy in these post-Epiphany Masses.

THE WEDDING-FEAST

Let us contemplate Jesus at Cana. There is so much meaning for us in this miracle. The young couple wanted Him and His Mother at their wedding breakfast. And He and His Mother wanted to be there — as He wants to be at every wedding, as He wants to be with every couple all their lives. That is lesson enough for us. But there are others. There was the thoughtfulness of both Jesus and Mary for the feelings and well-being of others. "The Mother of Jesus said to Him, 'They have no wine.' His Mother said to the attendants, 'Do whatever He tells you!' " It was thoughtfulness, not only for the feelings of the young couple who were saved from the embarrassment of not providing the wherewithal for the celebration, but also for the new disciples who had left all things to follow Him, perhaps without knowing too well why they did it. "This first of his signs Jesus worked at Cana; and he manifested his glory, *and his disciples believed in him.*"

But Cana is for the world. Christ was also thinking

of us. He worked this miracle for us too. And today in this celebration of that first of His miracles He wants to reveal His glory *to* us so that *through* us, as through the first Apostles, His glory may be made known to our world. Christ knows us better than we know ourselves. He knows how badly we need to be changed. He sees that already we have forgotten His Apostle Paul's advice at the beginning of the Church Year: "Put ye on the Lord Jesus Christ!" He sees that we opened our hearts to Him at Christmas and then closed them on New Year's Eve, forgetting all about Him. He knows our tendency to isolate ourselves from our neighbors and from the problems and cares of our world.

Therefore today He works this miracle for us, as much as to say: If I could change water into wine, I can change bread into My body and wine into My blood. And if I can make these miraculous transformations, I can also change you into an apostle, filled with My love for souls and for the glory of My Father. He takes the initiative now as He did then. But He cannot do it alone. He needs our help. "Fill the jars with water," He said to the attendants. They obeyed. It was a small thing He asked them to do, but the important point is that He asked them for their cooperation. And the water was made into wine, the best wine, rejoicing the hearts of the guests.

THOU HAST KEPT THE GOOD WINE

To us He says: "Fill the bread and wine that you offer at Mass with *yourself*, with your heart, your will, your whole being, and I will change you into Myself." We must not fear this change. It will rejoice us. It will give us a sense of being worth-while, and of doing worth-while work — none other than the work of Christ Himself. "Increase within us, we implore Thee, O Lord, the exercise of Thy power; so that, being nourished by Thy Divine Sacraments, we may be prepared to obtain out of Thy bounty that which they promise" (Postcommunion prayer).

The Eucharist, sacrifice and sacrament, is Cana all over again... and more. Through it we can welcome Christ into our lives, we can offer ourselves to His transforming power. Because of it we can come to realize what great things He has done and continues to do for our soul. It is the Eucharist that is "the good wine that He has kept until now" (Gospel).

After the wedding comes life together for the married couple. After the Cana of Sunday Mass comes the week in the world for all of us. In today's Epistle St. Paul gives directions for the community and family life in which our apostolate is to be worked out: "Let love be without pretense. Hate what is evil, hold to what is good. Love one another with fraternal charity... Be fervent in spirit, serving the Lord, rejoicing in hope... Be patient in tribulation, persevering in prayer. Share the needs of the saints, practising hospitality... Rejoice with those who rejoice; weep with those who weep. *Be of one mind towards one another.*" Following these directions will be a good test of our desire to be transformed into Christ.

1. Let the mercies of the Lord give glory to Him; and His wonderful works to the children of men. Praise ye the Lord, all His angels: praise ye Him, all His Hosts (Gradual and Alleluia verses)!

2. Shout with joy to God, all the earth: come and hear, and I will tell you, all ye that fear God, what great things the Lord hath done for my soul (Offertory verse)!

3. Thou hast kept the good wine until now (Gospel).

THIRD SUNDAY AFTER EPIPHANY

POWER AND GLORY

The Church cannot forget Epiphany. Today's Introit, Gradual, and Alleluia verses still speak of the majestic King whose manifestation to us at Epiphany foreshadows His coming again in power and glory at the end of time. "Adore God, all you His angels: the Lord hath reigned, let the earth rejoice" (Introit). "The Lord hath built up Sion, and He shall be seen in His majesty. The Lord hath reigned, let the earth rejoice: let many islands be glad. Alleluia" (Gradual).

But the Church does more than just cling to memories, precious though they be. She realizes that she has a long hard task to perform in preparing her children to meet this great King in judgment at the end of their lives. Therefore, after a prayer for the "right hand of God's Majesty" to be held protectingly over us, she proceeds to become very practical, which means that she shows us Jesus at work.

The Gospel contains two incidents: a leper comes to Jesus and begs to be healed. His prayer is imme-

69

diately granted. A centurion simply states his case: his servant is sick. Christ says: "I will come and heal him." But the centurion objects: "Lord, I am not worthy that thou shouldst enter under my roof; but only say the word, and my servant shall be healed."

Then Jesus marvelled. This man was a pagan. He knew little about God. But He was good, honest, fair, charitable, and humble. Above all, he believed that Jesus could and would help him. Christ's reaction to the incident is most interesting: "Amen I say to you, I have not found so great a faith in Israel. And I tell you that many will come from the east and from the west, and will feast with Abraham and Isaac and Jacob in the kingdom of heaven, but the children of the kingdom will be put forth into the darkness outside; there will be the weeping and the gnashing of teeth."

OVERCOME EVIL BY GOOD

We can bring this incident up to date. What Christ wants to tell us today is that we are not going to be saved by mere membership in the Church: many Catholics will lose their souls, while many others who have not had our advantages will be saved. What must we do? Like the centurion, we must recognize Jesus as *our God, our Savior.* We must come to Him in our troubles. We must be humbly grateful to Him for our gift of faith. AND WE MUST PRACTICE CHARITY! Charity after the manner of the centurion, who had at heart the welfare of the poor and sick. And charity in the sense of forgiveness of enemies.

70

Time and again in the Church Year Christ comes back to this essential virtue. Today through St. Paul He tells us: "Be not wise in your own conceits. To no man render evil for evil, but provide good things not only in the sight of God, but in the sight of all men... Be at peace with all men. Do not avenge yourselves, beloved..." (Epistle). Christians must be convinced once and for all that they simply cannot hate anyone and still be good Christians. We can hate sin, we can dislike systems, but we cannot hate sinners or misguided upholders of systems. "Vengeance is mine; I will repay, says the Lord. If thy enemy is hungry, give him food; if he is thirsty, give him drink... Be not overcome by evil, but overcome evil with good" (Epistle).

Human attitudes towards others, no matter who they be, that are full of hatred, desire for revenge, spite, and suspicion, choke Christ's action within us. He cannot take over in our lives unless He can get into our hearts. But a heart full of hatred and envy turns in on itself and locks the door from the inside. It is alone. It is unhappy. God is not there because God is Love.

CHRIST WORKING NOW

But our Lord wants to appeal more to our love than to our fear. He wants us to see Him as our Rescuer and our Redeemer. The leper and the centurion were not satisfied with their condition. So they went to Jesus, and they were overjoyed at His response to their distress. In Baptism and holy Penance the same Christ takes away the leprosy of sin from our souls. "The right hand of the

Lord hath wrought strength: the right hand of the Lord hath exalted me: I shall not die, but live, and shall declare the works of the Lord" (Offertory verse). In Confirmation He anoints us unto His own apostolate, commissioning us to carry on for Him. And in the Eucharist He feeds us with His Flesh and Blood.

"All wondered at these things which proceeded from the mouth of God" (Communion verse). We must learn to see Christ not only as an historical figure, acting in another age, but as *present to us* now in His Church. We must think of our confessions, our sharing in Mass and Holy Communion, our acts of charity to others, as personal contacts with the living Christ. Then we too will wonder at the things He does for us. And when we "wonder," that is, when we are in awe at the works of God, we are very close to His heart.

FOOD FOR THE WAY

1. The Lord hath reigned; let the earth rejoice: let many islands be glad (Introit).

2. Lord, if thou wilt, thou canst make me clean (Gospel).

3. Lord, I am not worthy that thou shouldst come under my roof; but only say the word, and my servant will be healed (Gospel).

FOURTH SUNDAY AFTER EPIPHANY

Note : The date of Easter varies. If it comes early this year, one or the other, or all, of the following three Sundays after Epiphany will be used next fall just before the Twenty-Fourth Sunday after Pentecost. In that event, however, just the Collect, Epistle, Gospel, Secret, and Postcommunion of these Masses will be used. The sung parts, that is, the Introit, Gradual, etc., will be taken from the Twenty-Third Sunday after Pentecost.

━━━━━

HIS DISCIPLES FOLLOWED HIM

"At that time Jesus got into a boat, and his disciples followed him" (Gospel). They followed Him willingly and eagerly. Then came the storm, and with it terror and despair. They wished they hadn't come. To make matters worse, their beloved Master seemed entirely unconcerned about their fate, for He kept on sleeping. So they went to Him and cried: "Lord, save us! We are perishing!"

And Jesus awoke. He said to them, "Why are you fearful, O you of little faith?" He then arose and rebuked the wind and the waves, and there came a great calm. And they wondered what manner of man this was that even the wind and the waves obeyed Him.

These were Christ's chosen ones. But apparently they were far from ready for their life work. This and many other miracles would not make them ready. They would not be fit of the apostolate until they came to realize that by themselves they were insufficient, that without Christ they were nothing (but trusting in Him they were secure), that union of will with Christ was all that mattered. They would not be ready until they had received the fullness of the Holy Spirit, the Spirit of Love, Fortitude and Zeal on Pentecost.

This Gospel contains the briefest history of the Church that we know of. Like her Master the Church has to go through the storm of a Good Friday death. Waves and tides of opposition assail her throughout her voyage across the seas of time. There are moments when her Captain Christ apparently sleeps, when the tempest seems about to swallow her up. But CHRIST IS STILL IN THE SHIP. "Why are you fearful, O you of little faith?" Easter will come, eternal Easter, when Christ will arise, rebuke the storm and the waves, and there will come a great calm.

OUR TEMPTATION

With that in mind we can see that today's Mass contains priceless lessons for modern apostles. We too are beginners in the game, we resemble the disciples in the boat to the very letter. Like them we willingly follow our Lord into the ship, into the apostolate. Then the storm breaks. Waves of opposition, apathy, ridicule, threaten us, bringing back memories of safety — memories of the old, selfish, but comfortable, days when the burden of the world's suffering was the exclusive concern of welfare workers, communists, and a few saints. The urge to give up, to despair, is the greatest temptation apostles of any age have to overcome. Human nature is so very weak.

But we are in Christ's ship, we are members of His Church which is held up by a powerful promise. The Church knows our weakness, but she also knows a cure for it. She can pray and have full confidence that her prayer will be heard. "O God, Who dost realize how difficult it is for us to stand against dangers too great for our weak nature, grant us health of mind and body, so that, by Thy help, we may be victorious over the sufferings caused by our sins" (Collect).

We have to come to know that worry about results, dismay over opposition, and inability to get things done indicate that we are perhaps trusting too much in our own efforts and not enough in the power of Christ's presence in the ship with us. In the apostolate self must disappear. This is not our work, this apostolate, but His. Therefore our prayer must always be the prayer of Christ at the moment when the waves seemed about to overcome Him: "Not my will, but Thine be done."

When we learn to trust Christ and to unite our wills to His, ready to accept *any* outcome, including even the complete destruction of our life's work, then there will

75

come a great calm over our lives. No storm, no opposition, will disturb us, for we are one with Him who has it in His power to command the winds and the sea. If there is apparent failure, it is His concern. Failure is most often like Good Friday. The grain of wheat has to go into the ground and die before it can bring forth fruit. The blood of martyrs is the seed of Christians. But Good Friday is the prelude to Easter Sunday. "Why are you fearful, O you of little faith?"

THE FULFILLMENT OF THE LAW

Therefore the one thing necessary in our Christian apostolic life is union with God through freely-given and loving consent to His holy Will. It is this consent, says Père Lochet, that makes us like unto Him and that makes us one with Him. This union with God is the soul of the apostolate. And it is this union with God that makes it possible for us to love our neighbor as he should be loved and thus "fulfill the Law" (Epistle). Without union with God — so that we love what and whom He loves — love of neighbor can become mere sentimental humanitarianism. Our apostolate is more than the improvement of the physical conditions of our environments — important as that may be. We want to improve conditions so that, as has already been pointed out, souls can more easily be brought to love God. "May Thy Gifts, O God, free us from the fascination of earthly things and ever give us new strength by their heavenly nourishment" (Postcommunion prayer).

FOOD FOR THE WAY

1. Thou shalt love they neighbor as thyself (Epistle).
2. Why are you fearful, O you of little faith (Gospel)?
3. What manner of man is this, that even the wind and the sea obey Him (Gospel)?

Note: If the calendar requires the celebration of the Fourth and Fifth Sundays after Epiphany at this time, the reader can find the explanation of these Masses at the end of the book, just before the Twenty-Fourth Sunday after Pentecost.

THE EASTER CYCLE

With Septuagesima Sunday the Easter Cycle of the Church Year begins. During this time the Church will celebrate the mystery of our Redemption. But we are only gradually led up to that tremendous event. The Septuagesima, or pre-Lenten season (three Sundays) makes us aware of our sinfulness and need of salvation. Lent (four Sundays) conducts us along the road of penance and self-denial and seeks to renew in us our baptismal integrity. During Passion Time (two Sundays) we contemplate Jesus the Man of Sorrows in the depths of His suffering, His passion, death, and burial. Then comes the high point of the year — Easter. During this entire season (five Sundays) we rejoice with all the joy of which the human heart is capable at the triumph and exaltation of our Head. "Death is swallowed up in victory." Finally come Pentecost and the Sundays after Pentecost (twenty-four) during which the seed of divine Life planted in during our baptismal renewal at Easter is supposed to grow and bring forth fruit unto the final harvest at General Judgment.

SEPTUAGESIMA SUNDAY

LIFE OR DEATH

Back in 1942 a public official described the American national war and defense effort as follows: "It is no joyride, no W.P.A. program. We are not playing for marbles. This is a matter of life or death."

Such a description of the life of a lay apostle in our times is too good to be forgotten. Today's Mass, especially the Epistle and Gospel, remind us sharply of the fact that we are not playing for marbles either. For ourselves and for our world, our "playing" is a matter of life or death — of the eternal kind.

There is first of all our responsability for our own spiritual development, the fulfillment of our own call to become perfect. St. Paul, model of apostles, does not mince words: if we are to win in the game of life, we must go into training as any athlete does. "I chastise my body, and bring it into subjection, lest perhaps after preaching to others I myself should be rejected" (Epistle). He again reminds us (as does Christ in the Gospel) that being called to the apostolate and being a Catholic is no guarantee of salvation. "For I would not have you ignorant, brethren, that our fathers were all under the cloud, and all passed through the sea, and all were baptized in Moses, in the cloud, and in the sea. And all ate the same spiritual food, and all drank the same spiritual drink... Yet with most of them God was not well pleased" (Epistle).

GO INTO MY VINEYARD

Then there is our responsibility for others. "The kingdom of heaven is like a householder who went out early in the morning to hire workers into his vineyard" (Gospel). He went out again at the third, the sixth, the ninth, and the eleventh hour. "Why do you stand here all the day idle? Go you also into my vineyard, and I will give you what is just." We cannot miss the point our Lord makes here: He cannot stand idleness anywhere. He wants workers. He needs workers to help Him save mankind. If any of the parables shows Christ's dependence on men for the continuing of His work of redemption, it is this one. He first invited us to work in His vineyard when He anointed and commissioned us at Confirmation. Today He repeats the invitation. We must work. And we must enlist others to work with us.

What is the work to be done? It is Christ's work — the consecration of the world to the Father. It is helping ourselves and others to recognize that the Father's glory is all that matters. This is no easy task, but "hard labor in the heat of the day" (Gospel). There are times when we feel the "groanings of death and the sorrows of hell" (Introit) surrounding us. But the follower of the Church Year knows what to do. He will call upon the Lord, and

80

the Lord will hear his voice from His holy temple. Praying with the Church, he cannot fail to see God as a "Helper in due time in tribulation: let them trust in Thee who know Thee: for Thou hast not forsaken them that seek Thee, O Lord. For the poor man shall not be forgotten to the end" (Gradual).

OUT OF THE DEPTHS

The Church is Christ. Christ is the Church. The Church Year is Christ's year, it is "Christ Himself who is ever living in His Church" (Pius XII). We are entering into the Easter Cycle of the Church Year during which the Church is going to celebrate the Passion and Death of our Lord. "From the depths I have cried to Thee, O Lord; Lord, hear my voice. Let Thine ears be attentive to the prayer of Thy servant" (Tract). This is Christ our Lord speaking (No stranger He to the groanings of death and the sorrows of hell); it is the Church; it is we ourselves; it is the world around us crying out for salvation.

During this period the Church will try to make us learn the outstanding lesson of our Faith — that there can be no joy for us, no results in our apostolate, *except* in realizing in our own lives the passion and death of Christ our Head. To our sin and ease-inclined natures this prospect is distasteful, perhaps terrifying. Yet we know that we need purification, that our self-love (and our tendency to stand around all the day idle) has to be rooted out. But living into the Passion and death of our Lord is really no more terrifying than any Mass. For the

Mass is Christ's death *and glorification*, as it is also ours if we give our best to its celebration.

After the first part of today's Mass convinces us that we must accept Christ's invitation to work in His vineyard and to enter into His coming Passion; after we have sacrificed our own wills in the offering of bread and wine, we shall receive the Victim of the Sacrifice as our Food. It is only giving like that — total generous gift of self — that can help us to see in the last analysis that work in the vineyard is the most satisfying work of all. "It is good to give praise to the Lord, and to sing to Thy name, O Most High" (Offertory Verse).

The Communion verse sounds forth with the fore-taste of victory that will be ours when the sacrificial "Mass" of our life in the vineyard is over. God will "make His face to shine upon His servant and will save us in His mercy. Let me not be confounded, O Lord, for I have called upon Thee" (Communion verse).

FOOD FOR THE WAY

1. I will love Thee, O Lord, my strength: the Lord is my firmament, and my refuge and my deliverer (Introit).
2. If Thou shalt observe iniquities, O Lord, Lord, who shall endure it? For with Thee is propitiation, and by reason of Thy law I have waited for Thee, O Lord (Tract).
3. Even so the last shall be first, and the first last; for many are called but few are chosen (Gospel).

82

SEXAGESIMA SUNDAY

HE THAT HATH EARS

The sower went out to sow his seed. The seed fell along the wayside, on rocks, amongst thorns, and some fell on good ground. We know what happened to the seed in each case. 'He that hath ears to hear, let him hear" (Gospel)! CHRIST IS SPEAKING TO US!

Christ Himself is the Sower, and the seed is the word of God. The seed has no future when planted along the wayside (in souls which become the crossroads of this world's flighty values). In rock soil (souls that are fickle and lack perseverance) the seed cannot take roots. It is hardly more successful in ground covered with thorns (souls deadened by the cares and riches and the illicit pleasures of this life). The seed can grow and bear fruit only in soil that has been well fertilized and stirred up by the plows and drags of mortification.

"The seed is the word of God." There is more in the word "word" then meets the eye. It does mean literally what it says: instruction, teaching, doctrine. But Christ sows more than His teaching in the soil of our hearts. Recall His words: "I have come that they might have LIFE and have it more abundantly." Christ is the Life.

Christ is the Seed. He plants Himself in us. Some of this Seed falls on the wayside, some on rocks, some among thorns, and some in good soil.

SEED OF GLORY

"What kind of soil am I?" No serious-minded person can dodge that question after listening to today's Gospel. A sincere glance over the past will undoubtedly make us admit to a good deal of familiarity with the wayside, the rocky, and the thorny soil our Lord talks about. Shallowness of mind, selfishness, complacency, and the cares, riches and pleasures of this life — all have contrived to exhaust the soil of our hearts and to make that soil a hopeless lodging place for Christ the Seed to take root and germinate.

When soil is abused, it becomes worn out. Soil needs fertilizing, moisture, constant plowing and dragging. So also the soil of man's heart. The stirring up and fertilizing of the soil of our hearts take place every year during Lent. During this holy season the entire Mystical Body, which means us, gives itself over to the plows and harrows of self-denial. Weeds of self-love and slavery to the demands of the flesh are rooted out. And the rain of holy reading and prayer moistens our soul, making us eager for the sowing of the Seed.

And then of course the stirring up of the soil takes place at every Holy Mass if we know what we are doing. There we offer bread and wine as symbols of ourselves. But what do we do when we offer ourselves? If the offering is honest, we give our *wills* to God. "Please,

Lord, you take over in my life," we say to Him... and we mean it.

It is easy to say "Not my will but Thine be done." But most of the time when we say it, there is a secret hope in our hearts that God will not really take us up. To give up even that secret hope, to put oneself absolutely into God's hands so that our will mirrors His — if we do that, then we are the best kind of soil, for then we are co-victims with Christ. It takes many a Mass and a lot of living to arrive at that degree of generosity; so we must not be discouraged. "Perfect Thou my goings in Thy paths, O Lord" (Offertory verse).

This is sacrifice, the stirring up of the soil. Holy Communion is the seeding. "Some seed fell on the good ground... and yielded fruit a hundredfold." The Eucharist is the SEED OF GLORY. That is why we can say: "I will go in to the altar of God, to God Who giveth joy to my youth" (Communion verse). The altar of God gives joy. But the altar is the place of sacrifice where God accepts the gift of our wills. Perhaps we shall have to wait until Easter to understand the connection between the altar of sacrifice, between mortification's harrowing, and the hundredfold yield of the Seed of Glory and Peace and Goodness that will then be ours. At Easter our Offertory prayer will be answered, and God will "show forth His wonderful mercies, because we have learned to trust in Him."

IN LABOR AND HARDSHIPS

In today's Epistle St. Paul tells us the story of his life. In order to defend himself against his enemies, he related how he was beaten, stoned, imprisoned, ship-wrecked, starved, deceived by false friends, upset by dissension among his converts.

He also tells how he was caught up into paradise and heard secret words that man may not repeat; how, to keep humble, God gave him a "sting of the flesh." He besought God to relieve him of the temptation and heard those words that will console Christian apostles till the end of time: "My grace is sufficient for thee, for strength is made perfect in weakness." This was the kind of life God wanted Paul to life. It was this apostolic, difficult, dangerous life that made him a saint.

Almost the first words Paul spoke to our Lord at his conversion were: "Lord, what wilt Thou have me do" (Acts of the Apostles 9:6)? At that moment he became good soil for the Word of God. He gave himself to Christ, and Christ planted Himself in him. Paul brought forth fruit a hundredfold.

God alone can count the conversions St. Paul was responsible for in his own lifetime, as well as the souls in whom he sowed the seed of Christ's word since then through his Epistles. The Mystical Body has grown in extent, depth, and wisdom because Paul was fertile soil for Christ's seeding. What happened to Paul can happen again. "We humbly ask Thee, O Almighty God, that we, who have been refreshed by Thy Sacraments, may serve Thee worthily by a life well pleasing to Thee" (Postcommunion prayer).

FOOD FOR THE WAY

1. Arise, O Lord, and cast us not off to the end: why turnest Thou Thy face away, and forgettest our trouble? Arise, O Lord, help us and deliver us (Introit)!

2. Gladly will I glory in my infirmities, that the strength of Christ may dwell in me (Epistle).

3. I will go in to the altar of God: to God Who giveth joy to my youth (Communion verse).

QUINQUAGESIMA SUNDAY

ATTITUDES TOWARDS LENT

To many modern folks, Lent does not mean a thing. Life goes on as before. They eat, work, play, drink, suffer... and live for the next weekend. If they think of Lent at all, they see it only as a relic of bygone days, a primitive torture device that our world has happily outgrown.

To others — perhaps most of us — Lent means a dreary time of penance and mortification, a sort of necessary evil that has to be lived through stoically like a reducing diet and then forgotten with a sigh of relief for another year. We simply do not like it. The words of today's Gospel are fulfilled in adherents of both of these attitudes: "They understand none of these things... they understood not the things that were said." Perhaps the true Christian attitude towards Lent will emerge from a study of this Mass.

WE GO UP TO JERUSALEM

What do we do during Lent? The ordinary Catholic practices some mortification. If we are old enough, we

88

follow the Church's laws of fast and abstinence. If not we may give up eating between meals, sweets, smoking, drinking, movie-going. We will go to Mass more frequently during the week, pray more, do more spiritual reading, practice works of mercy, such as visiting the sick and aged. This is all very good *if* we know what it all adds up to and if we do these things from the right Christian motive. It all adds up to *dying with Christ;* and the right motive is *love for Him* and *willingness* to die with Him.

Here is the way it is. Lent is the yearly renewal of our Baptism. According to St. Paul, Baptism is dying with Christ in order to rise with Him. "We are buried together with Him by Baptism unto death; that as Christ is risen from the dead by the glory of the Father, so we also may walk in newness of life" (Romans 6:3).

It is hard for us to get excited about our Baptism: it happened so long ago, and we had so little to say about it. But now we can have something to say. Now we can consent freely to what Christ did for us when He plunged us into His death. By our Lenten self-denial we freely consent to go along with Jesus when He says to us in today's Gospel: "Behold, *we* are going up to Jerusalem, and all things that have been written through the prophets concerning the Son of Man will be accomplished. For he will be delivered to the Gentiles, and will be mocked and scourged and spit upon; and after they have scourged him, they will put him to death; and on the third day He will rise again."

"Unless you take up your cross and follow Me, you cannot be My disciple," Christ says to us. What He did, we must do, each of us. "Lord, that we may see" this necessity!

So Lent for us must be a dying to self. Dying to self implies changing our life, conversion, turning away from self. This is not an agreeable prospect for our fun-loving, easy-going natures. But "the third day He shall rise again!" We cannot rise with Christ at Easter, we cannot expect new Life and Christlike Easter joy without first dying with Him by dying to self during Lent.

THE GREATEST OF THESE

The conversion that we face also implies a renewal of our attitude towards our neighbor, our family, school, parish, community — the whole Mystical Body. For the individual alone, Lent can be quite unbearable. But Lent is not for the individual alone. It is the business of the whole family of God. We pray: "Be Thou gracious to *our* prayers, O Lord, *we* implore Thee, and, having released *us* from the heavy chains of sin, protect *us* from all adversity" (Collect). We are all in it together. But how little do we feel our real oneness with one another! And yet we know from our Lord's teaching that love for one another is as necessary as taking up our cross and following Him.

It would probably not be too strong to say that the purpose of Lent is the development of charity within us, substituting love of God and neighbor for love of self in our souls. If we should know all mysteries and all knowledge, if we should have all faith so that we could move mountains, and have not charity, we are nothing.

"Charity is patient, is kind. Charity does not envy, is not pretentious, is not puffed up, is not ambitious, is not self-seeking, is not provoked to anger... bears with all things, believes all things, hopes all things, endures all things... So there abide faith, hope, and charity, these three: but the greatest of these is charity" (Epistle).

Charity alone makes community life possible. Charity is the greatest need among Catholics today. The most austere mortifications — fasting, praying, alms-giving — are all vain shadow-boxing if our love for God and for our neighbor is not an active, driving force in our life. Loving God in Himself, and loving Him in our neighbor — that is our goal in Lent and in life. When the Lent of life is over, love alone will remain.

"Thou art the God that alone dost wonders" (Gradual). In the last analysis, success in Lent and in life depends on our growth in the right attitude towards God. Christ is God-centered, the Church is God-centered. The Liturgy and the apostolate are God-centered. WE MUST BE GOD-CENTERED. Then we will have true community life with charity binding us together. And if we are God-centered, no Lenten program or self-denial will frighten us. On the contrary, we will "Sing joyfully to God... We will serve Him with gladness and come in before His presence with exceeding great joy, knowing that the Lord He is God... and *we are His people* and the sheep of His pasture" (Tract).

FOOD FOR THE WAY

1. Be Thou unto me a God, a protector, and a place of refuge, to save me... In Thee, O Lord, have I hoped,

91

let me never be confounded: deliver me in Thy justice, and set me free (Introit).

2. The greatest of these is charity (Epistle).

3. Jesus, Son of David, have mercy on me (Gospel)!

FIRST SUNDAY OF LENT

THE LORD THY GOD SHALT THOU ADORE

"He shall cry to Me, and I will hear him; I will deliver him, and glorify him; I will fill him with length of days" (Introit). This is one of the rare Sundays of the year in which God speaks to us directly in the opening words of the Mass.

God is speaking of His Son, of His Son's Mystical Body the Church, of us who are members of that Church. What He says is that He is the Supreme Lord, that we are His creatures; that He loves and protects us and desires intimate union with us. Christ in the Gospel insists on the supremacy of God: "The Lord thy God shalt thou adore, and Him only shalt thou serve." This is the great lesson of Lent. Lent wants to convince us of but one thing: that God alone must matter in our lives. "Remember, Man, that thou art dust, and to dust thou shalt return."

God is Creator. We are creatures. We must not tempt the Lord our God by reversing the truth and setting up ourselves, our human needs and desires, to be adored. We must not seek our souls' satisfaction in bread alone, but must feast on the "word that proceedeth from the mouth of God" (Gospel).

THE DAY OF SALVATION

It was to drive home to mankind the basic truth of God's utter supremacy that Christ lived, suffered, died. It is to repeat and solemnly impress us with this truth that the Church celebrates Lent. "We entreat you not to receive the grace of God in vain" (Epistle).

There is no greater grace for man than to feed on this truth. Our world has forgotten it and is therefore the prey of despair. But it is not too late. "For God says, 'In an acceptable time I have heard thee, and in the day of salvation I have helped thee.' Behold, now is the acceptable time; behold, now is the DAY OF SALVATION" (Epistle)! Lent is the day of salvation for us, for our Church. If we can bring ourselves to see God as our God — adorable and lovable — and to direct our whole life to Him, then it will also be a day of salvation for our world.

Hence there is no reason in the year that is more important. We need not fear that admitting God's supremacy will lessen our dignity as men. To see God as our supreme Lord and Master is to see Him aright. For it is to see Him through Christ's eyes as our Father Who says to us: "You shall cry to Me, and I will hear you... I will give My angels charge over you, to keep you in all your ways. In their hands they will bear you up, lest you dash your foot against a stone... Because you have hoped in Me, I will deliver you; I will protect you because you have known My Name... I am with you in tribulation. I will deliver you, and I will glorify you; I will fill you with length of days, and I will show you My salvation" (Tract).

THE DEVIL'S PART

So we have God pleading with us to return to Him. But we also have the devil seeking to keep us in our present self-adoring condition. For, if God is interested in Lent, the devil is, too — hating God and us as he does. The devil does not think Lent is a very good idea at all. And therefore he will tempt us to gloom at the prospect of six weeks of self-denial. He will tempt us to pride at the mortifications we undertake. He will tempt us to uncharitable thoughts and words against our neighbor, knowing that a heart at odds with its neighbor is farthest from its God.

But the devil's most powerful attack on us will be from the vantage point of the demands of our bodies. He knows that Almighty God "by the fasting of the body curbs our vices, elevates our minds and bestows virtue and reward" (Preface). Our lower nature dislikes all suppression. It objects to the curtailment of food, drink, sense-pleasure. Satan's argument goes like this: Forty days of mortification are too much. You will never make it. You are not strong enough. You work too hard as it is. You had better not even start. Besides, you don't really need it. Mortification is old-fashioned. Eat, drink, have fun. Use God's good things now. (We can be pretty certain that, when the devil says "use," he means "abuse.")

We answer with Christ: 'Not by breads alone does man live, but by every word that comes forth from the mouth of God" (Gospel). Man is body and soul. The whole man must be fed. He who tries to live without feeding his soul is in danger of committing soul-suicide.

He tempts God. He becomes miserable, and there is every danger that he will become bestial.

THE WORD FROM THE MOUTH OF GOD

The food required by our soul is Holy Communion, the Divine Victim of the Sacrifice. And it is PRAYER. Our prayer must not be mere lip-prayer thoughtlessly run through. It must be a constant effort to make our own the *spirit of the words.* What is this spirit? It is the HOLY SPIRIT — the same Holy Spirit Who led Christ into the desert and who now wishes to lead us through this Lenten fight to victory with Christ at Easter. The prayer that contains this Holy Spirit is Christ's prayer. Christ's prayer is the Church's prayer, Holy Mass and Divine Office. This is "the word that comes forth from the mouth of God."

To grasp and to live on the spirit of the Church's prayer is to penetrate into the very mind of Christ and to have one's soul filled with that mind. By this spirit and by the holy reception of His Sacrament we will have new strength, we will be changed from our old life, we will be brought into union with God. And then we shall be able to fulfill our Lord's desire: "The Lord thy God shalt thou worship and Him alone shalt thou serve."

FOOD FOR THE WAY

1. Now is the acceptable time; now is the day of salvation (Epistle)!

2. Lord, Thou art my protector and my refuge: in You will I trust (Tract)!

3. The Lord will overshadow thee with His shoulders, and under His wings thou shalt trust: His truth shall compass thee with a shield (Communion verse).

SECOND SUNDAY OF LENT

Lent is a world-wide retreat for the whole Church, and Christ is the Retreat-Master. Our life often seems so confused. We wander about aimlessly, sometimes on high ridges of joy, sometimes in low valleys of gloom. We wonder what life is all about. Most often we do not care. Retreats propose to put order into the chaos of life. The retreat of Lent is especially a time of spiritual renewal. Christ our divine Retreat-Master gives us a definite goal to aim at in the texts of today's Mass.

"Jesus took Peter, James and his brother John, and led them up a high mountain by themselves, and was transfigured before them. And his face shone as the sun, and his garments became white as snow... And behold, a voice out of the cloud said: 'This is My beloved Son, in whom I am well pleased; hear him' " (Gospel).

Jesus transfigured. This is HOLINESS, this is SANCTITY, the God-life in Him visibly shining through His human body. This is the goal of *our* life, the purpose of Lent: transfiguration into Christ.

Father Daniélou in his book *The Salvation of the Nations*, well describes ordinary human reactions to holiness. We find it tremendously desirable and attractive (Peter wanted to stay there on the mountain with Christ the rest of his life). But at the same time we experience a feeling of fear and almost of being rejected by God, because contact with this holiness makes us so aware of our fundamental impurity and unworthiness (Peter fell on his face in great fear).

SORROW

Our Retreat-Master knows these human reactions to the ideal He presents to us, and He provides us accordingly with appropriate texts with which to express what we have in our hearts. "The troubles of my heart are multiplied, deliver me from my necessities, O Lord. See my abjection and my labor, and forgive me all my sins" (Gradual). "O God, Who seest how weak we are, guard our interior and exterior life, that our body may be defended against adversity and our mind cleansed of evil thoughts" (Collect).

All the Lenten Masses, this one in particular, give daily voice to our grief over past infidelities and our need for God's help in purifying ourselves. "Remember, O Lord, Thy compassion and Thy mercies. To Thee I have lifted up my soul" (Introit). But sorrow for sin is tempered with another human reaction: desire for union with God, desire to love and praise Him: "Give glory to the Lord, for He is good: for His mercy endureth forever. Who shall declare the powers of the Lord? Who shall set forth all His praises? Remember us, O Lord, in the favor of Thy people; visit us with Thy salvation" (Tract).

Perhaps in the past we have seen this Gospel of the Transfiguration of our Lord as belonging to another world, having nothing at all to do with us. But it has everything to do with us. For transfiguration is what Christianity (and Lent and life) is all about. Christ was born, lived, suffered, died and rose again in order to give glory to His Father *and* to transfigure mankind. Hence our vocation in life, God's call to each of us, is to identify ourselves with the transfigured Christ, to give ourselves over to Him so that He may transfigure us.

THE WILL OF GOD

Jesus wants us to do more than just contemplate holiness. He wants us to achieve it. In the Epistle He tells us through St. Paul: "This is the will of God, your sanctification... For God has not called us unto uncleanness, *but unto holiness in Christ Jesus our Lord.*"

God wills that His Son's Church, and that each of us members of that Church, be holy. We must not say: "He doesn't want much!" God has ways of getting what He wants. He made us saints once before when He saw to it that we were baptized. He can complete the work during this and following Lents. And He will complete it if we can only bring ourselves to say: "It is my will too."

When God wills sanctity, and we will sanctity, we have sanctity. It is as simple as that. Or perhaps it is not so simple, especially that second condition, for it means giving ourselves over to Him so that He may freely work in us. We can utter our will for sanctity in every holy

Mass when we offer ourselves to God at the offertory...
and above all when we give free rein to Christ, Calvary's Victim, our Communion Food. The Mass daily
re-enacts Christ's Transfiguration on our altars. There is
no better means for personal transfiguration than the
Mass.

"I will meditate on Thy commandments, which I
have loved exceedingly; and I will lift up my hands to
Thy commandments, which I have loved" (Offertory
verse). God's commandment, His will, is our sanctification. Through Lent, through mortification, through
"meditation on His commandments," and through alms-
giving, to our Easter transfiguration into Christ: that is
the ideal that gives purpose and meaning to our life. It
is that commandment that we must love exceedingly.

Lent conducts us up a high mountain. Its summit is
Easter, which is to be Christ's tranfiguration and glorification and our own. At Easter we shall say with St.
Peter: "Lord, it is good for us to be here." And God
our Father will say to us: "You are my beloved sons in
whom I am well pleased."

But mountain climbing is for men and women in
good condition. We cannot climb if we are out of shape
because of over-indulgence in pleasures of the body, or
weighted down by the cares and pleasures of the world.
It may be that some of us are exempt from the Church's
laws of fasting. But no one has a right to exempt himself from the *spirit* of the fast: that binds everyone who
is sincere about fidelity to his Christian vocation. There
must be some mortification. The Lenten program must
hurt if it is to be profitable in lightening us for the climb.
"Humbly do we pray Thee, O Almighty God, that we

whom Thou dost refresh with Thy Sacraments, may also serve Thee by a *manner of life that is pleasing to Thee*" (Postcommunion prayer). Self-denial is that kind of manner of life.

FOOD FOR THE WAY

1. To Thee, O Lord, have I lifted up my soul: in Thee, O my God, I put my trust; let me not be ashamed (Introit).

2. Lord, it is good for us to be here (Gospel)!

3. Understand my cry: harken to the voice of my prayer, O my King and my God: for to Thee will I pray, O Lord (Communion verse).

THIRD SUNDAY OF LENT

EYES TOWARDS THE LORD

We can have a better understanding of today's Mass if we recall and make our own the dispositions of the early-Church catechumens. They were awaiting Easter, not only as the day of Christ's victory, but also as the day of their own triumph over Satan which would be theirs as soon as they were baptized.

"My eyes are ever towards the Lord: for He shall pluck my feet out of the snare: look Thou upon me, for I am alone and poor. To Thee, O Lord, have I lifted up my soul; in Thee, O my God, I put my trust" (Introit). Thus did the catechumens pray. Thus do we pray, too, for we do not forget that this is our Mass as well as theirs, and that we also look forward to breaking the devil's hold on us through our Easter baptismal renewal.

WALK IN LOVE

After a beautiful prayer for both catechumens and faithful, the Church read them an instruction from St. Paul that gave them an ideal for their future life as intimate followers of Christ. "Be imitators of God, as very dear children and walk in love, as Christ also loved us and delivered himself up for us an offering and a sacrifice to God to ascend in fragrant odor" (Epistle).

So far, the Church seemed to say to the catechumens, you have struggled hard: parents, relatives, friends have perhaps tried to get you away from Christ. The old pre-conversion sinful pleasures still seem alluring. You have probably not yet broken clear. You know your past standard — avarice, passion, dishonesty. You were in darkness, you were on the road to eternal darkness. But now the light of the divine Sun is about to rise over you. "Walk, then, as children of light, for the fruit of the light is in all goodness and justice and truth."

Immediately the catechumens replied: "Arise, O Lord, let not man (our fallen human nature) be strengthened. To Thee have I lifted up my eyes... Behold as the eyes of servants are on the hands of their masters. And as the eyes of the handmaid are on the hands of her mistress: so are our eyes unto the Lord our God, until He have mercy on us. Have mercy on us, O Lord, have mercy on us" (Gradual and Tract).

The Church next proceeded to give her prospective children an example of the power of her Head Christ in His campaign against Satan, His and their enemy. He cast out the devil from the dumb man, and immediately the dumb man spoke. Our Lord's victory in this Gospel is a pre-view of His victory at Easter, and a glimpse of His victory in the souls of the catechumens when He would drive out the devil from them in holy Baptism.

We can imagine the force with which Jesus drove home those dramatic words: " He who is not with me

104

is against me; and he who does not gather with me scatters... Blessed are they who hear the word of God and keep it" (Gospel). We can also imagine the catechumens' firm desire really to keep Christ's word and live His way of life when they would become Christians. Most of them did keep that word, some at the cost of their own blood.

The catechumens left the church at this point with a holy envy in their hearts for the faithful who were even then carrying their gifts to the altar, singing the Offertory psalm as they went: "The justices of the Lord are right, rejoicing hearts, and His judgments are sweeter than honey and the honeycomb: for Thy servant keepeth them."

SELF-EXAMINATION

This week we observe the half-way mark in Lent. Today should be a day of serious self-examination for us all. At our Baptism Christ drove the devil from us and took possession of us. We in turn chose Him and His way of life. He asked us: "Dost thou renonce Satan... and all his works... and all his pomps?" Through our sponsors we answered yes, and we renewed those baptismal vows with a free and personal oath of fidelity at our Solemn Communion.

Now we are no longer catechumens. We have received the Light. We have been incorporated into Christ. He has lived in us and we in Him. But what is our condition now? Do we walk as children of the Light, as imitators of God, as His most dear children? Or are we all too familiar with those sins mentioned in the Epistle: uncleanness, covetousness, serving the idol of our own will? He who is not with me is against me. Has this Lent meant any change at all in our lives? Monsignor Hellriegel says: "At the end of Lent one is either more vitally incorporated into Christ, or he is less a Christian." On Easter we will either be better than we were before Lent, or we will be worse. We cannot stay neutral.

Incorporation into Christ means that Christ should direct our every thought and act. It means that our daily life (like His and Mary's) should be worshipful, charitable, dedicated to the will of the Father in the perfect fulfillment of the demands and duties of our present vocation. Above all, our life must be sacrificial. We must be convinced that there can be no growth of Christ in us, no walking as children of light, if we have not the spirit of sacrifice, penance, mortification. Some devils "can only be cast out by prayer and fasting," Christ insists (Matthew 17:20). And the Lenten Preface puts it this way: "By corporal fasting, Thou, O God, dost curb our vices, elevate our minds, and bestow virtue and reward." This is the law of God. It admits no exceptions.

"He who is not with me is against me." These words of Christ are terrifying. We have only one choice: Christ or Satan. We can have Christ living in us or be friends of the devil. These two are deadly enemies. We must choose which one to follow. There can be no compromise. "He who does not gather with me scatters."

FOOD FOR THE WAY

1. To Thee, O Lord, have I lifted up my soul: in Thee, O my God, I put my trust (Introit).

2. Blessed is the womb that bore thee, and the breasts that nursed thee (Gospel).

3. Thy altars, O Lord of hosts, my King, and my God: blessed are they that dwell in Thy house, they shall praise Thee for ever and ever (Communion verse).

FOURTH SUNDAY OF LENT

REJOICE

"Rejoice and be glad, you that were in sadness: that you may exult and be suckled plentifully with the consolations she offers you" (Introit, Knox translation). Violet, the penitential color, gives way to vestments of rose; flowers deck the altar; the organ plays; and the Church greets us with one of her most joyous salutations.

The Church has good reason for her joy. Easter is near: glorious Easter with its freedom for her children from the bonds that the devil and sin have wrapped around their souls, Easter, the feast that foreshadows the freedom she will enjoy at the end of time when this world will have loosened the ties that hold her down, and she will have become at last the heavenly instead of the earthly Jerusalem she now is. 'I rejoiced at the things that were said to me: We shall go into the house of the Lord" (Gradual). Going into the House of the Lord which is heaven is certain for the Church. It is not quite so certain for us, but we need not fear if we live on the spirit of the Church's prayer.

THE HOLY CITY

This Mass is filled with references to Jerusalem the Holy City. For the Jews, Jerusalem was the chosen city of God. He dwelt there in His magnificent temple. To go up to Jerusalem was for them the greatest of joys. To be in exile from it filled them with gloom, as the Psalmist illustrates: "Upon the rivers of Babylon, there we sat and wept: when we remembered Sion... How shall we sing the song of the Lord in a strange land? If I forget thee, O Jerusalem, let my right hand be forgotten. Let my tongue cleave to my jaws, if I do not remember thee: If I make not Jerusalem the beginning of my joy" (Psalm 136). "He shall not be moved for ever that dwelleth in Jerusalem. Mountains are bound about it: so the Lord is round about His people, from henceforth, now and forever" (Tract).

For us Christians Jerusalem is the CHURCH OF CHRIST, His Mystical Body, wherein God is more than round about us, but is rather in us. The Church is that Jerusalem which is *from above* (Epistle) and which will lead us back up there. We live in this Holy City now, but "we have been in sorrow" (Introit). We have not sufficiently realized our oneness with Christ and with one another in this blessed City. We have not thought enough of bringing others to citizenship in it. We have not yet sufficiently realized our oneness with Christ and with one another in this blessed City. We have not yet been sufficiently purified from our sins to enjoy fully the freedom of *new Life* which will come to us in the renewal of our Baptism, nor the heavenly peace and happiness that are essential to the Easter atmosphere of the Holy City.

TRUE JOY

"I rejoiced at the things that were said to me: We shall go into the house of the Lord." Our joy in our Easter Jerusalem will be mostly spiritual. It will be based on full citizenship in the house of the Lord. It will be the joy of the "tribes that go up, the tribes of the Lord, to praise Thy Name, O Lord" (Communion verse).

True joy is not so much a thing of the body as it is of the spirit. We know that from experience. The joy that comes from sense pleasures passes away, leaving only empty hearts still yearning to be filled. *Real joy is freedom from having to depend on earthly things such as food, drink, amusement.* "Joy is the special reward of mortified lives. A spirit of penance which enables us to endure the minor trials of life causes us to rise above them. We breathe a supernatural atmosphere in which such troubles have no power to weigh us down, and thus we attain the freedom with which Christ has made us free" (Lady Lovat).

The conclusion is obvious: there can be no true and lasting joy without self-denial. Before we can take joyous possession of our joyous Easter freedom, we must go into the door of death-with-Christ that opens to us in the days of Lent that remain. Freedom for our Savior came only after He had died and spent three days in the tomb. We members of Christ cannot separate ourselves from Him. Our giving up of pleasures, our daily work and fidelity to the big and little demands of our vocations; our striving to substitute patience, charity, and understanding for envy, anger, dislike — all this is our sharing in Christ's death. Our Easter joy will be in proportion to our willingness to die with Christ now.

BREAD OF LIFE

We will be wise if we join our daily dying-to-self to the Passion and death of Christ re-enacted on our altars at Holy Mass. Fasting and Eucharist always go together. We saw on the first Sunday of Lent that, after forty days of fasting, followed by Satan's temptations, angels came and ministered to Christ. We do not have to wait forty days. As we fast, denying ourselves material food, our Lord feeds us with the Bread of the strong, His own Body and Blood. "Make the people recline," He said (Gospel). "The men therefore reclined, in number about five thousand. Jesus then took the loaves, and when he had given thanks, distributed them to those reclining; and likewise the fishes, as much as they wished." We share in the fulfillment of which this Gospel is the promise.

"I am the bread of life... I am the living bread which came down from heaven. If anyone eat of this bread he shall live forever. Unless you eat the flesh of the Son of Man, and drink his blood, you shall not have life in you... He who eats my flesh and drinks my blood has everlasting life, and I will raise him up on the last day" (John 6:48-56).

"Praise ye the Lord, for He is good: sing ye to His Name, for He is sweet" (Offertory verse). These are our sentiments as we offer ourselves to God in this Mass, and as we live out that offering in the coming important days of Christ's and our sacrifice. "Do Thou, we beseech Thee, O Lord, give heed and be appeased by the sacrifices here before Thee, that they may be of profit to our devotion and salvation" (Secret prayer).

FOOD FOR THE WAY

1. I rejoiced at the things that were said to me: We shall go into the house of the Lord (Introit).

2. This is indeed the Prophet who is to come into the world (Gospel).

3. Praise ye the Lord, for He is good: sing ye to His name, for He is sweet: whatsoever He pleased He hath done in heaven and in earth (Offertory verse).

PASSION SUNDAY

THEY TOOK UP STONES

" 'Which of you will convince me of sin? If I speak to you the truth, why do you not believe me? He who is God hears the words of God. The reason why you do not hear is that you are not of God.' 'If I glorify myself, my glory is nothing. It is my Father who glorifies me, of whom you say that he is your God. And you do not know him, but I know him.' They therefore took up stones to cast at him; but Jesus hid himself, and went out from the temple" (Gospel).

We come now to the climax of this great drama of Redemption. The Divine Hero enters into open and dangerous conflict with His enemies, and, although His hour is not yet come, it is evident that His enemies will soon triumph, at least temporarily. "Often have they fought against me from my youth. Let Israel now say: often have they fought against me from my youth. But they could not prevail over me: the wicked have wrought upon my back. They have lengthened their iniquities: the Lord Who is just will cut the necks of sinners" (Tract).

The Christ of the Passion speaks to us from the texts

of this Mass. The suffering Savior wishes to take complete possession of the next two weeks. But more than all else, He wants to take possession of us, of our minds, our hearts, our whole beings. "Judge me, O God, and distinguish my cause from the nation that is not holy; deliver me from the unjust and deceitful man. For Thou are my God and my strength" (Introit).

WHAT THE PASSION IS TO US

Are we mere onlookers at the Passion as we would at the execution of a condemned man? In showing us the Suffering Savior, the Church does want to move us and make us repent our sins that have made such a pitiful spectacle of the Son of Man. But the Church wants much more than a stirring-up of our emotions. She wants us to be grateful to Him and to reform our lives.

Above all the Church wants us *to relieve in ourselves the Passion of Christ.* "Have this mind in you which was also in Christ Jesus" (Phillipians 2:5), she says to us. Be sacrifice-minded, she will insist time and time again. The Church desires that our contemplation of the agonizing Christ inspire in us the will to be co-priests and co-victims with Him. Nor is this to be just a pious exercise of our imagination.

We know that Baptism identified us with Christ. "All we who have been baptized into His death. For we were buried together with him by means of Baptism into death, in order that, just as Christ has arisen from the dead through the glory of the Father, so we also may walk in newness of life" (Romans 6:3-6). Therefore Christ's Passion belongs to us and we to it. We have a

114

right to say with St. Paul: "With Christ I am nailed to the cross: it is now no longer I that live, but Christ lives in me" (Galatians 2:20).

But how specifically can we relive the Passion? "Not my will, but Thine be done," Jesus said, and then He went forth to the way of the cross, to Calvary, to death. Have *this* mind in you. "O Lord, teach me to do Thy will" (Gradual). To relive the Passion we must also say: "Not my will, but Thine be done, O Lord." We must say it and mean it. Then we must go out into the way of the cross which is our apostolic life in the world and *do God's will*, whatever the cost to our human will in pain and effort and tears.

But the Passion of Christ is not an end in itself. Even in the most solemn and tragic moments of these next two weeks, the Church remembers that Easter will inevitably come. The image of the Man of Sorrows is before our eyes. But our minds must not stop at the Man of Sorrows idea. We must see in Him above all the Victor who overcame death so that we might live. Moreover, we must see ourselves as victors in and with Him. In and with Him we overcome the world's threat to our supreme right to Christian joy. In other words, we overcome the littleness, the stinginess, the selfish mediocrity of our lives. We overcome sin. "Today if you shall hear his voice, harden not your hearts" (Psalm 94:8). The voice of Christ speaks to us from these Passiontide Masses inviting us to die with Him now so that we may live with Him in holy Easter joy. "He who is of God hears the words of God... Amen, amen, I say to you, if anyone keep my word, he will never see death" (Gospel).

PASSION AND APOSTOLATE

There is no more important lesson for modern lay apostles than the lesson of the Cross. The lesson is this: that as Christ defeated Satan, glorified the Father and brought new Life to mankind by His sacrifice, so by our sacrificial union with Him lived out, by our prayer and our action, is that redeeming work of the Savior made available and effective in our world. We must die with Him. The grain of wheat must fall into ground and die before it can bring forth fruit. This is beautifully indicated in the Preface of the Holy Cross which we say these holy days: "It is truly meet and just... to give thanks to Thee, Eternal God: Who didst establish the salvation of mankind in the wood of the cross, that whence death came into the world, thence a new life might spring."

Our apostolic work may not show results. There may be apparent failure. There will always be opposition. That is not the point. Willingness to do God's will, oneness with that divine will in all things and dying with Christ means doing our best now and *leaving the rest in His hands*. The fruit will come when He wants it.

"Hail, O Cross! thou only hope of man" (Vespers hymn). The Cross was man's only hope. It still is man's only hope. But where the Cross is, Easter cannot be very far off. Through the Cross to glory!

FOOD FOR THE WAY

1. Deliver me from my enemies, O Lord, teach me to do Thy will (Gradual).

2. I will confess to Thee, O Lord, with my whole heart: I shall live and keep Thy words: enliven me according to Thy word, O Lord (Offertory verse).

3. This is My Body which shall be given up for you; this cup is the new covenant in My Blood... Do this as often as you drink it, in remembrance of Me (Communion verse).

PALM SUNDAY

CONTENTS OF HOLY WEEK

"Brethren: have this mind in you which was also in Christ Jesus... He humbled himself, becoming obedient to death, even to death on a cross. Therefore God also has exalted him" (Epistle).

The CROSS, the Savior dying on it, the burial, the resurrection: that was Jesus' life *then*. It was humble obedience to God's will leading to death and being rewarded with magnificent exaltation. It was a passage from death to life. Good Friday and Easter Sunday were a single unbroken action.

The Catholic ALTAR, the same Savior renewing His death, His burial, His resurrection: that is Christ's life *now*. It is His death and resurrection become our passage from death to life. Fruitful participation in Holy Week depends on our will to make the content of Holy Week a reality in ourselves.

Let us recall that we are one with Christ. St. Paul tells us "All you who are baptized into Christ, have put on Christ... You are all one in Christ Jesus" (Galatians 3:27-28). Therefore St. Thomas could say: "Through

118

baptism man is *incorporated into the passion and death of Christ;* wherefrom it follows that the *passion is communicated to the baptized person as if he himself had suffered and died.*

Christianity for us must not be just a way of life, a kind of label impressed upon us. It must be a living experience, a suffering-with Christ in imitation of Mary and John beneath the cross. It is humbling ourselves, becoming obedient to God and our vocation even unto the death of the cross. It is a constant attitude of mind that expresses itself in Christ's words: "Father, if this cup cannot pass away, unless I drink it, Thy will be done" (Communion verse).

We know from our past life that, even though we have been plunged into the Passion of Christ by Baptism, we can and do close our hearts to the workings of that Passion within us. We do not die to sin. We remain enamoured with our pet attachments to impatience, tyranny over others, anger, distrust, envy, spiritual laziness, intemperance in eating and drinking. We are uninterested in Christ, the worst insult of all. In us His words are verified: "I looked for one who would grieve together with Me, and there was none: I sought for one to comfort Me, and I found none; and they gave me gall for My food, and in My thirst they gave me vinegar to drink" (Offertory verse). We look upon Holy Week as an imposition, an unwelcome interference in our work and play. But it should be rather a precious opportunity for each of us to open up the way for Christ's *mind* and His *will* into our souls.

MARTYRS WITH CHRIST

On Palm Sunday palms are blessed and distributed. The palm is the ancient symbol of *victory through martyrdom*. Hence, when we hold out our hand to receive the blessed palm, we do something very great: we ask for martyrdom with Christ. The visible hand-held-out is an outward sign of our inward desire and will to accept and make our own the cross, the death, the victory of the Prince of Martyrs which He re-enacts for us during these days of grace.

"Can you drink the cup of which I am about to drink?" He asks us as He asked the first apostles (Matthew 20:27). "Yes, Lord, we want to," we answer. And then we show forth the sincerity of our desire by active, intelligent, generous living into the words, the actions, the signs of our Holy Week services. We accept the palm of the victorious passion, resolving with Christ's help, to carry it throughout the week, throughout our life. During the year the piece of palm tacked up in our rooms and houses can remind us of what we are and what we did: we are martyrs with Christ. We asked for it.

"Celebrate these feasts, plunge into them, live them" (Father H. A. Reinhold). This is the only formula that will make the Passion and Victory of Jesus really personal to us. To use this formula is to become Christ. With Him we are nailed to the Cross. He lives in us... We live in Him.

"It behooves us to *glory* in the cross of our Lord Jesus Christ: in whom is our salvation, life, and resurrection"

(Introit, Holy Thursday). "Hosanna to the Son of David! Blessed is he who comes in the name of the Lord" (Gospel)! The Passion is the blessed, the *happy* Passion, because it alone saves. Through our sharing in it, we are going to share in and live on the Life in Christ's risen body. We, too, are going to pass from death to life, even as the Hebrew children by the blood of the paschal lamb passed through the Red Sea waters of salvation to the opposite shores leading to the Promised Land. "We adore Thy Cross, O Lord: and we praise and glorify Thy holy resurrection: for behold, by the wood of the Cross, joy came into the whole world" (Good Friday antiphon).

SUGGESTIONS

Shy away from sentimentalism during this Holy Week. Do not be content with pity for the suffering Savior. It passes away too quickly, leaving us unchanged in heart. We should strive rather to *penetrate into the mind of Christ by our personal mental prayer* so as to share His trust in the Father, His love for men, His desire to unify the world, His hatred of sin.

Each of us has a part in Christ's Passion this year. Our missals are our script. We must know our script. Practice it. Prepare it beforehand. The fruit of Christ's Passion will come to us in proportion to our intelligent and ardent participation in this holy Liturgy, together with our will to purify our hearts of selfishness and pride.

The fruit of the Passion will be *Easter Joy, New*

Life, in us. Therefore, we thank our Lord and promise Him to live in that Life, to increase it in the coming year. "I am the vine, you are the branches. He who abides in me, and I in him, he bears much fruit; for without me you can do nothing. If anyone does not abide in me, he shall be cast outside as a branch and wither; and they shall gather them up and cast them into the fire, and they shall burn" (John 15:5-7). "How good is God to Israel, to them that are of a right heart" (Gradual)!

FOOD FOR THE WAY

1. Have this mind in you which was also in Christ Jesus (Epistle).

2. O God, my God, look upon me: why hast Thou forsaken me? Far from my salvation are the words of my sins" (Introit).

3. My people, what have I done to thee? or in what have I grieved thee? Answer me (Good Friday, Improperia).

4. Behold the wood of the Cross, on which hung the Savior of the world. Come let us adore (Good Friday, Adoration of the Cross).

EASTER SUNDAY

EASTER FOR CHRIST

DEATH IS SWALLOWED UP IN VICTORY! The central Figure in the Easter Mass is the Savior in triumph. "I have risen, and am still with you" (Introit).

This is what we have been aiming at and working for: Easter, this greatest of feasts, this resplendent celebration of our Redemption, this glorious victory of our Lord, this foretaste of eternal happiness.

The Lamb redeems the sheep; And Christ the Sinless
      one hath
To the Father sinners reconciled. Together life and death
In a strange conflict strove; The Prince of Life, Who died
NOW LIVES AND REIGNS" (Sequence).

On days like this the human tongue is almost help-less to express sentiments worthy of the wondrous event that is celebrated. But why use human words when we can throw heart and soul into the Church's expressions — so full of joyous meaning today? "This is the day which the Lord hath made: let us be glad and rejoice therein. Give praise to the Lord, for He is good: for His mercy endureth forever. Christ, our Passover, has been sacrificed" (Gradual). "Glory be to God on high! We praise Thee. We bless Thee. We adore Thee. We glorify Thee. We give Thee thanks for Thy great glory... O Lord Jesus Christ, O Lord God, Lamb of God, Son of the Father, Who takest away the sins of the world" (Gloria)! "You are looking for Jesus of Nazareth, who was crucified. He has risen, he is not here. Behold the place where they laid him" (Gospel).

The joy in the Redeemer's own heart vibrates through His Church's prayer today, taking possession of the minds and hearts of those who have truly died to self and to sin in the Lent just passed. "Holy, Holy, Holy, Lord God of Hosts, the heavens and the earth are full of Thy glory."

EASTER FOR US

In the midst of our joyous celebration the Church does not allow us to forget what Easter should mean to us. This meaning is to be found in the Epistle. But to grasp it, we must first recall a Jewish Passover custom.

On the Feast of the Passover (which, through the sacrifice of a lamb, commemorated the deliverance of the Chosen People from Egypt — foreshadowing our deliverance from hell through the sacrifice of the Lamb of God), it was customary to remove all old leaven (yeast) from the houses. The purpose of this removal was to symbolize the removal of sin from their lives, because yeast causes fermentation and was considered a sign of corruption.

124

Accordingly, in the Epistle St. Paul tells us: "Purge out the old yeast from your lives (Do away with your unnatural grasping after material riches, your love of unlawful pleasure, your pride, uncharity, injustice). In the future let us keep festival, not with the old yeast, nor with the yeast of malice and wickedness, but with the unleavened bread of sincerity and truth."

We do not want our Savior's Passion and death to be in vain. Nor do we want our own Lenten death to sin to be in vain. Sin must never again gain hold over us. We are finished with it. We are Christ's and our lives are henceforth hid with Christ in God. But past experience teaches us how greatly we need this Secret prayer: "Receive, we implore Thee, O Lord, the prayers of Thy people, together with our offering of sacrifice; so that *what we have begun on this Feast of Easter may by Thy grace become a healing remedy unto life everlasting.*"

We rejoice, we give praise, we give thanks. "It is truly fit and just... to praise Thee, O Lord, at all times, but more gloriously at this time when Christ, our Pasch, was sacrificed. For He is the true Lamb, Who has taken away the sins of the world; Who, by dying, has overcome our death, and by rising has restored our life" (Preface).

THINGS THAT ARE ABOVE

"Have this mind in you which was also in Christ Jesus," so were we told during the Passion season. Should we not also put on the mind of the risen Savior?

125

The mind of the risen Savior is this: "If you be risen with Christ, seek the things that are above" (Epistle of Holy Saturday).

Having the mind of the risen Savior and seeking the things that are above means only one thing: growth in detachment from things of the earth so that these do not absorb our attention to the point of making us forget the one thing necessary. Growth in detachment means constant, year-long, life-long *sacrifice*. Yes, we can talk about sacrifice at Easter. We can talk about it especially at Easter, because it is now that we can realize better than at any other time the value of sacrifice; for today we are enjoying the fruits of sacrifice: its new Life, its freedom, its peace, its joy. Yes, Lord, it is good for us to be here!

"I have risen, and am still with you," He says to *us*. He is with us always. He is with us every day in the mystery of His life, death, and resurrection which is the Mass. Here at Mass we can be with Him in a daily, weekly, yearly growth out of slavery to self into the ever more invigorating air of that freedom which is truly from above.

Here at daily and weekly Mass we can grow in the Life that floods us today. Look about in the fields and forests. Everywhere we can see new life. Life demands growth, whether it be natural life or supernatural. Our divine Life wants to develop in the months to come. In autumn the natural life that now has the appearance of buds and green sprouts will show itself in the form of ripened fruits, ready to be gathered into the cellars and granaries. What about our new Easter Life? It too will develop if we abide in Christ, if we tear up the killing weeds of selfishness, if we nourish it constantly with the Bread of Life, the Eucharist. "Pour forth upon us, O Lord, the spirit of Thy love, and in Thy goodness make us to be of one mind and heart, whom Thou hast fed with Thy Easter Sacrament" (Postcommunion prayer).

FOOD FOR THE WAY

1. I have risen, and am still with Thee, alleluia (Introit).

2. Give praise to the Lord for He is good, for His mercy endureth for ever (Gradual)!

3. Christ, our Passover, has been sacrificed, alleluia: therefore let us keep festival with the unleavened bread of sincerity and truth (Communion verse).

FIRST SUNDAY AFTER EASTER

EFFECTS OF EASTER

"PEACE BE TO YOU! As the Father has sent me, *I also send you*" (Gospel). Today's Gospel covers eight days. Notice what our Lord did: on the very night of His resurrection, the first thing He thinks of, upon seeing the apostles again, is to send them forth carrying the resurrection and its fruits into their world. They are to go out and be witnesses to His glorification.

In the months just passed, we too have died and risen with Christ. To us, too, He says: "As the Father has sent me, I also send you." Why are we sent? What do we have that our Lord wants our world to receive through us? Today the Church prays with us "that we may always keep the spirit of Easter in our life and conduct" (Collect), in other words, that we may always show forth the effects of Easter in our life.

Recall how, on the Second Sunday of Lent, we saw our Lord splendidly transfigured on Mount Tabor. His garments were white as snow, and His face shone as the sun. St. Paul told us then: This is what Lent is supposed to do to you. At Easter you are to be transformed into Him, you are to become saints. Well, Easter has come. We have climbed the mount of the Transfiguration; today we stand on the summit with Christ. Perhaps we are not wholly transfigured, we are not yet saints. But we have tried to die to self, we have made our Easter confession, and the radiant Life of the Risen Christ pulses through us. We are "born of God" (Epistle). We are living branches of Christ the true Vine.

A WORLD TO OVERCOME

The greatest crime we could commit now would be to go back to our pre-Lenten state of sin and selfishness. But almost as great a crime would be that if ignoring and forgetting what we are by virtue of Christ's presence within us. It would be a disaster for us... and for our world. Remember His words: As the Father has sent me, I send you. "He who is born of God *overcomes the world*" (Epistle).

What is this world we are to overcome? It is first of all anything that destroys our oneness with Christ, anything that would substitute the devil's way of thinking for Christ's — pride, hatred, forgetfulness of God. In another sense, we who are transfigured, who are born of God, are to overcome the men of this world; we are to win them to Christ, so that He can transform them too.

We are born of God. Christ dwells in us. But it seems it is not enough to possess divine Life. This life in us must become operative in us through FAITH. "Who is he that overcomes the world if not he who believes that Jesus is the Son of God" (Epistle)? If anyone ever proved by deed his right to our faith, it is Christ. "Put in thy finger, and see my hands, and bring hither thy hand, and put it into my side, and be not faithless, but believing" (Gospel).

MY LORD AND MY GOD! These words of the Apostle Thomas are words for modern apostles, words that can make apostles, that can spark the victory over the world that is in our hands. He suffered and died. But He rose again from the dead, so that we might have the Life of God within us. I have risen, and am still with you. "I am the Vine, you are the branches. Abide in me, and I in you." MY LORD AND MY GOD!

THOSE WHO ARE BLESSED

"These things are written that you may believe that Jesus is the Christ, the Son of God, and that believing, you may have life in his name" (Gospel). These things are also written that by our believing, others, because of us, may also have life in His name.

Christ is our all. By His resurrection, He is the source of our divine Life, He is the content of our faith, He is the nourishment both of our Life and our faith. For both faith and Life have to be renewed constantly. Otherwise the old sluggishness, apathy, and defeatism will return. The food of our faith is the Eucharist. Hence we pray: "O Lord, our God, we beseech Thee to make this holy Sacrament a remedy for us both in the present and the future, since thou hast given it as the sure defence of our salvation" (Postcommunion).

And the food of our faith is prayer. The kind of

prayer that dwells on the victory of Christ, rejoices in it, is grateful to Him for it. The prayer that best fulfills these requirements is the Liturgy — the Mass and the Sacraments. At every Mass He stands before us saying: "Peace be to you. As the Father has sent me, I also sent you." We do not see Him as the apostles did. But "Blessed are they who have not seen, and yet have believed" (Gospel). These words are addressed to us. Christ was thinking of us, of us who are supposed to do for our world without seeing Him what Thomas did for his world after he had put his hand into the Savior's side.

We do not see. But we believe that He is in His Church, we believe that the Mass is His redeeming act in our midst, we believe that He sends us into our world, laden with His Life, His Vision, His Truth. We believe all this because our daily, weekly, yearly living and praying with Him in His Liturgical Year have built up our faith and made us truly blessed, not because we have seen, but because we have believed. "This is the victory that overcomes the world, our faith" (Epistle).

FOOD FOR THE WAY

1. Rejoice to God our helper: sing aloud to the God of Jacob (Introit).

2. Bring here thy finger, and see my hands; and bring here thy hand, and put it into my side; and be not unbelieving, but believing (Gospel).

3. MY LORD AND MY GOD! (Gospel)!

SECOND SUNDAY AFTER EASTER

SHEEP GOING ASTRAY

"I am the good shepherd. The good shepherd lays down his life for his sheep" (Gospel). With these words our Lord sums up His whole life and His relation to us. "I know mine and mine know me."

A good shepherd knows each of his sheep individually. He understands them, is acquainted with their habits and weaknesses. He realizes that they lack a sense of direction; and so he takes it upon himself to guide them to the best pastures and the coolest waters. And because he knows and loves his sheep, he does not hesitate to give his own life to save them from harm.

To a human race wandering about like sheep without a shepherd, the prey of the wolves of hell, starved for want of nourishing food, there came a shepherd, the Son of God. He guided His sheep, fed them in heavenly pastures, fought for their eternal life against the wolves, and gave His own life to save theirs. "Greater love than this no one has" (John 15:13). "By his stripes you were healed," St. Peter tells us in the Epistle. "For you were as sheep going astray, but now you have returned to the shepherd and guardian of your souls. »

132

These are the facts of Christ's life, the facts also of Lent and Easter this year. Jesus, our Good Shepherd, gave His life for us, His sheep, but more than that, He arose triumphantly from death, so that *He could continue to be our Shepherd*, since we still need Him. We still flirt with those persons and things that would destroy our souls, still break our legs on the rocks of sin, and still get caught in the thorns of materialism. "O God, Who, by the humility of Thy Son, hast lifted up a fallen world, grant perpetual happiness to Thy faithful ones, and since Thou hast rescued them from the perils of eternal death, bring them likewise to the realization of eternal joy" (Collect).

GREEN PASTURES

"The Lord ruleth me: and I shall want nothing. He hath set me in a place of pasture... He hath converted my soul" (Psalm 22).

When it comes to knowing what is good for them, sheep are not as stupid as they seem. They know enough to flock to their shepherd, especially at mealtime, because they know he will not fail them.

Our Good Shepherd, Christ, takes care of all our wants just as faithfully. All we have to do to be saved is to run after Him, cluster around Him, and eat of the Food He has prepared for us. Mealtime for us is Holy Mass. Mass is the greenest of pastures to which our Shepherd leads us. Here we can fix our eyes on Him, gather around Him, and hold out our hands to receive from Him the Food we need to strengthen the bond between Him and us. "O God, my God, to Thee do I watch at the break of day: and in Thy Name I will lift up my hands, alleluia" (Offertory verse). We know what the Food is. "I am the bread of life... I am the living bread that has come down from heaven. If anyone eat of this bread he shall have life forever; and the bread that I will give is my flesh for the life of the world" (John 6:48-53).

"I know mine, and mine know me." The word *know* has depth to it. Knowledge implies union between the knower and the one known. The knower possesses the one he knows and at the same time gives himself to him. At any rate, that is the way Christ knows us.

Compared to His knowledge of us, our knowledge of Him is pretty imperfect. It needs constantly to be improved, because there is no love without knowledge; and our Lord's main idea in this parable is to show His love for us so as to attract our return love for Him. How can we improve our knowledge of Christ? "The disciples *knew Him in the breaking of bread*" (Alleluia verse). At Emmaus, when the disciples saw Jesus bless and break bread in the inn, their eyes were opened, and they recognized Him as the One who had instituted the Holy Eucharist at the Last Supper. They saw Him as their Savior, their Lord, their Good Shepherd. Thenceforth their lives belonged to Him.

Christ "breaks bread" for us at every Mass. At Mass we can know Him, for there we can identify ourselves with Him. We can run to Him at the offertory, joining our wills to His, giving ourselves to Him with humble and loving confidence. Then the exchange takes place... and the union between Him and us. He offers us with

Himself to the Father; and the Father then gives Him back to us as the Food of our soul. "I know mine, and mine know me."

OTHER SHEEP I HAVE

"And other sheep I have that are not of this fold. Them also I must bring, any they shall hear my voice, and there shall be one fold and one shepherd" (Gospel). In the glow of love for Christ aroused in us by the main part of this parable, we are apt to pass over too lightly this last phrase. But these words are essential to our Lord's line of thought. So also is the apostolate essential to our vocation as sheep of Christ.

As long as our world has pagans who know Him not at all; as long as it has Christians, separated from Christ's visible shepherd in Rome, who know Him only partially; as long as it has Catholics who know Him only superficially, *the desire of Christ's heart for one fold and one shepherd must haunt us*. "In this we have known the charity of God, because He laid down His life for us: and we ought to lay down our lives for the brethren" (1 John 3:16). How can we say we know Him, how can we say we love Him, if we are uninterested in, if we do nothing about, if we do not sincerely pray for, Christ's most heartfelt desire — that of unity among men? He laid down His life for us. We must lay down our lives for the brethren. "Christ has suffered for us, leaving you an example that you may follow in his steps" (Epistle).

But the parable of the Good Shepherd is more than

a beautiful lesson for us. Today we *celebrate* His being-our-Shepherd and our being-His-sheep. We rejoice in this truth. "The earth is full of the mercy of the Lord, alleluia... Rejoice in the Lord, ye just" (Introit). We rejoice in Him, we praise Him, we thank Him, and in this tribute of love we find the grace and strength to be faithful, obedient, and apostolic.

FOOD FOR THE WAY

1. I am the Good Shepherd: and I know Mine, and Mine know Me (Alleluia verse).

2. O God, my God, to Thee do I watch at the break of day: and in Thy Name I will lift up my hands, alleluia (Offertory verse).

3. And other sheep I have that are not of this fold. Them also I must bring... and there shall be one fold and one shepherd (Gospel).

THIRD SUNDAY AFTER EASTER

STRANGERS AND PILGRIMS

The Church cannot get Easter off her mind; and we can hardly blame her. Easter has meant everything to her — victory, joy, peace. In that Feast of Feasts she has had a glimpse of the Eternal Easter, a sight so over-whelming that today, after three weeks, she is still forced to cry out: "Shout with joy to God, all the earth, alleluia; sing ye a psalm to His Name... Make His praises wonderfully resound" (Introit).

But today's Mass contains a new note. The Church remembers that she and her members are *pilgrims* living in exile in a non-rejoicing, realistic, largely pagan world that for the most part rejects most spiritual, other-worldly, eternal values. She knows this world for what it is: it can be a lovely world, but it can also be very dangerous for her children, depending on the use they make of it.

The Church loves the spiritual implications of the word "pilgrim." A pilgrim is a wanderer, a stranger, in a foreign land. He sojourns in the foreign land for a little while. Then, his mission accomplished, he goes back home. Meanwhile, he never forgets his real home and longs for it always.

In the Epistle St. Peter tells us that we are pilgrims and strangers. As such, he says, "refrain yourselves from carnal desires which war against the soul." It is always a timely warning, because, like some of the medieval pilgrims to the Holy Land, we are often tempted to take up permanent residence abroad, get ourselves entangled in eathly connections to such an extent that we forget about our home.

MODERATING EARTHLY DESIRES

The most difficult task we face in our pilgrimage of life is to keep a proper balance. There is the temptation on the one hand to despise created things and this world's happiness, and on the other to see them as the be-all and end-all of man's life. Friendship, love, beauty, food, drink, music — all these are from God. Therefore, they are good. They can remind us of their Creator, make us grateful to Him, stimulate our appreciation of Him and thus help us to arrive more easily at our heavenly home.

But these things can also become the occasion and cause of our downfall if we allow them to absorb our attention so exclusively that we have no time and no relish for God and our final goal with Him. If we lose sight of the fact that we are made for eternal union with Him in heaven, our true home, there is great danger that we will become pagan worshippers of the false idol of self. Hence, the appropriateness of today's Secret prayer: "By these mysteries, O Lord, confer upon us the grace *to restrain our earthly desires, so that we might learn how to love the things of heaven."*

Restraining earthly desires can only mean one thing: self-denial and detachment — giving up the use of God's good things from time to time *out of love for God.* (The motive must be love for Him. Any other motive, such as pride, or hatred of God's good things, would insult Him and do us little good). This is the one way that will permit Christ to become active in our lives. He cannot live and grow in an un-mortified soul, a soul that prefers self to Him.

Christ is always our model. He also was a pilgrim. In order to get back home, Christ suffered, died, and rose from the dead. Just as "it behooved Christ to suffer these things, and so to enter into his glory (Alleluia verse), so does it behoove us. There is no other way.

Mortification becomes hateful and distasteful to us when we think of it as being done by ourselves alone. But we are not alone. Christ is in us. "I am the vine, you are the branches." He is our Life. Hence Christian mortification is simply letting Him grow in us to the degree that we "reject what is opposed and follow what is becoming to His name" (Collect).

But our Lord in us *insists* that we do not despise our world. It is good. It can reflect the Father's beauty, goodness, and fertility. Christ died in order to consecrate this world more and more to the glory of the Father. We must *live and die* unto that end. In the world, though not of it, we are to behave well among our fellow-citizens, and by our good example and apostolic action draw them to Christ. We are to be subject to human laws and governments, to honor all men, love the

139

brethren, fear God, "that, whereas they speak against you as evildoers, they may, by the good works they shall behold in you, glorify God in the day of visitation" (Epistle). "The Lord has sent redemption to His people" (Alleluia verse); but that redemption is in our hands. We have to deliver it.

A LITTLE WHILE

Christ-in-us desires more than mortification. He wants us to become men and women of praise as He was. Our true vocation as other Christs is to adore and praise God; for that is the life in our heavenly homeland — a life our Lord wishes us to begin now. "Praise the Lord, O my soul; in my life I will praise the Lord: I will sing praises to my God as long as I shall be" (Offertory verse). There are so many things we do not fully understand. We do not understand pain or evil. We do not understand Christ-in-us. But if we throw ourselves heart and soul into the Liturgy of Praise which Christ offers us Sunday by Sunday, all things will become clear.

There is no danger of our becoming earthbound and pagan if we allow Christ-within-us thus to grow in our lives. There may be suffering, hardship, sorrow. "A little while, and now you shall not see me." The "little while" is our life on earth, in this exile. But He has gone to prepare a place for us. "And again a little while and you shall see me... I will see you again, and your heart shall rejoice: and your joy no man shall take from you" (Gospel). We have reason to cry: "Shout with joy to God, all the earth!" We have reason to rejoice.

140

FOOD FOR THE WAY

1. Shout with joy to God, all the earth... Make His praises wonderfully resound (Introit)!
2. It behooved Christ to suffer these things, and so to enter into His glory (Alleluia verse).
3. Praise the Lord, O my soul, in my life I will praise the Lord: I will sing to my God as long as I shall be (Offertory verse).

FOURTH SUNDAY AFTER EASTER

WONDERFUL THINGS

"It is expedient for you that I depart. For if I do not go, the Advocate will not come to you; but if I go, I will send him to you" (Gospel).

These are key words in today's Mass. But do we realize how important this promise of our Lord is for us? Do we see it as a promise made to *us*? Christ first made that promise to the Apostles. It was fulfilled on the first Pentecost when the Spirit of the Lord filled the whole earth.

Hundreds of years have passed since then, and the world-wide spread of the Catholic Faith is evidence that the Holy Spirit has not been idle since that time. He is in the Church today. He is in us, St. Paul tells us: "Do you not know that you are the temple of God and that the Spirit of God dwells in you? If anyone destroys the temple of God, him will God destroy; for holy is the temple of God, and this temple you are" (1 Corinthians 3:16-17). In us as in the Church, He works quietly so that often we take His presence for granted. But He is none the less active and effective.

Here is some evidence: the fact that there are priests offering Mass, dispensing the sacraments and preaching; that there are convents filled with self-sacrificing sisters, praying, teaching, nursing; that there are lay men and women, young and old, doing works of mercy among the poor, and working in the apostolate wherever they may be — all this proves that the Holy Spirit is still at work in the Church. For these are works of love, and are therefore works inspired by the Holy Spirit, the Spirit of Love.

Another proof of the presence of the Holy Spirit in the Church is the fact that we celebrate this Mass of the Fourth Sunday after Easter and come forth from it more solidly established as partakers of the Divine Nature (Secret prayer), filled with firm resolutions to live up to our great dignity by worthier lives. And if we feel convinced in reading or singing the Introit and other parts of this Mass that "God has done wonderful things" (Introit) to Christ, to the Church, and to us in the Easter just passed, we can thank the Holy Spirit for the gratitude we feel. "Alleluia, alleluia. The right hand of the Lord hath wrought power; the right hand of the Lord hath exalted me" (Alleluia verse).

HOW WE NEED THE HOLY SPIRIT

Nevertheless, Christ's promise still holds for us. It is expedient that He ascend to the Father in the coming feast of the Ascension so that He can send us the Holy

Spirit. For we need the Holy Spirit this year as much as the first apostles needed Him. First of all we need Him for ourselves. Listen to the prayer He has us pray today: "O God, Who dost make the faithful to be of one mind and will, grant that we, Thy people, may love what Thou dost command and desire what Thou dost promise; so that, amid the changing things of this world, our hearts may be fixed where true joys are to be found." We ask for the grace to love what He commands and to desire what He promises. He commands that the world should listen to His Son and obey His Son's new laws of love for one another. May we love that command, follow the Son's laws, and do all in our power to help their fulfillment! And He promises the Holy Spirit. Grant that we may desire Him. If we do not desire Him, He will never come to us. Just to ask ourselves if we are truly joyous now is to know that our need for the Holy Spirit is really critical. Among the changing things of this world our hearts will be fixed where true joys are to be found only when we give those hearts over to the Spirit of Love and allow Him to unite us to God.

HOW THE WORLD NEEDS THE HOLY SPIRIT

Our world also needs the fulfillment of our Lord's promise. Our world will never become Christian unless and until Christians are fired by the Holy Spirit to Christianize it. They are supposed to be the leaven at work in the mass of mankind. There would never be any apostolate without the Holy Spirit. He was necessary for the beginnings of the Church. He is necessary today.

"When He has come, He will convict the world of sin, and of justice, and of judgment" (Gospel). These are mysterious words: but they take on real meaning in our cooperation with the fulfillment of the promise of the Paraclete. If we allow the Holy Spirit to possess us and then go out and live among men, the world seeing us, seeing our joy and sincere zeal, will become uneasy and restless. The Holy Spirit in a person is holiness, and holiness is always disturbing. Our world will see the falseness of its way of thinking and will then be ready to receive in its turn "the perfect gift which is from above, coming down from the Father of Lights, with whom there is no change nor shadow of alteration" (Epistle), so that its heart too may be fixed where true joys are to be found.

So we must desire strongly, and prepare ourselves earnestly for the coming of the Spirit to us. St. James in the Epistle tells us how to prepare: "Let every man be swift to hear, but slow to speak and slow to wrath. For the wrath of man does not work the justice of God. Therefore, casting aside all uncleanness and abundance of malice, with meekness receive the ingrafted word, which is able to save your souls."

"Shout with joy to God, all the earth: come and hear, and I will tell you, all ye that fear God, what great things the Lord hath done for my soul" (Offertory verse). We can shout with joy for what Christ did for us at our Baptism and at the renewal of our Baptism this Easter. We can shout with joy again and always for what He does to us at every Mass wherein He makes us to share

His Godhead. But above all, we can shout with joy in anticipation of His best of all gifts, that Gift which is truly from above which will come to us not many days hence: His own Spirit, the Spirit of Love.

FOOD FOR THE WAY

1. Sing ye to the Lord a new canticle, alleluia; for the Lord hath done wonderful things, alleluia (Introit).

2. Christ, having risen from the dead, dies now no more, death shall longer have dominion over Him (Alleluia verse).

3. When He, the Spirit of truth, has come he will teach you all truth (Gospel).

FIFTH SUNDAY AFTER
EASTER

BLESSED BE THE LORD

"I came forth from the Father and have come into the world.

Again I leave the world and go to the Father" (Gospel).

In this shortest but most sublime of all auto-biographies, our Lord sums up His whole life. He was born of the Virgin Mary, lived, taught, suffered, died, and rose from the dead. But He also founded a Church in which He promised to be present all days and to which He bequeathed a Liturgy that would have the power to re-enact His life and work.

We are members of His Church. We have joined ourselves to His wonder-working Liturgy these past six months during which we have seen and heard wonderful things. For unto us a Child was born. The Word was made flesh and dwelt among us, and we saw and shared in His passion and death. But we also beheld His glory. And so with full hearts we cry out today: "O bless the Lord our God, ye Gentiles, and make the voice of His praise to be heard: Who hath set my soul to live, and hath not suffered my feet to be moved: blessed be the Lord, Who hath not turned away my prayer, nor His mercy from me, alleluia (Offertory verse).

DOERS OF THE WORD AND THE WORK

He came into the world alone: "I came forth from the Father and have come into the world." But by that coming He took possession of us. Now we belong to Him. "Again I leave the world and go to the Father." We remain. But He will come again. And the last time He comes, at our death or at the Last Judgment, He will say: "We leave the world and go to the Father." We must prepare for that.

There is so much to be done before we are ready to accompany Him. First of all, there is the obligation of being true to Christ by being true to ourselves, to our nature as redeemed members of Christ. We have often heard Christ's word. But more than that, He who is the Word, God's Son, was made flesh in us, dwells in us. Hence St. James tells us that we are to be doers of the word and not just hearers, deceiving ourselves and forgetting what manner of men we are.

We are one with Him who is Religion itself, with Him whose life was an uninterrupted act of worship of the Father and of merciful love for and service of man. We are not to be forgetful hearers of that work of religion, but doers as He was.

148

"He who has looked carefully into the perfect law of liberty and has remained in it, not becoming a forgetful hearer but a *doer of the work*, he shall be blessed in his deed" (Epistle). We say we love the Liturgy. We love the chants of our Sunday Masses, the Collects, Epistles, Gospels. Christ through St. James tells us: Beloved, be doers of the *word* and the *work*, not hearers only. Which means that our Lord wants us to be careful about two things: first that we really do the worshipful work of Christ, enter into it with all the mental and physical faculties and powers we possess. We are matter and spirit, soul and body. The whole of man, not just the mind, has a part in religion. "If we want to keep young Catholics in the Church, we must let them share her life and not be mere spectators. If we want them to become dynamic apostles, our ceremonies must help them to become conscious of the meaning of Christianity" (Abbé Michonneau). The Liturgy is supposed to sanctify and unify us. Perhaps in the past we have been too much hearers and not enough doers.

Secondly, being doers of the Word and the Work means that our lives during the week be worshipfully concerned about the glory of God and the spiritual and physical condition of our neighbors. "If anyone thinks himself to be religious, not restraining his tongue, but deceiving his own heart, that man's religion is vain. Religion pure and undefiled before God the Father is this: to care for orphans and widows in their tribulation, and to keep oneself unspotted from this world" (Epistle). It would be hard to improve on St. James in this characterization of what the Christian life ought to be.

Being a doer of the Word and the Work is not a task for weaklings. No one knew this better than Christ, and no one better than He could tell us what to do about our insufficiency: "If you ask the Father anything in my name, He will give it to you" (Gospel). *Anything* we ask *in Christ's name* will be granted. "Hitherto you have not asked anything in my name: (Is He right?) Ask, and you shall receive, that your joy may be full."

Our Lord wants us to pray as individuals for our daily needs. God is our Father. A father wants his children to ask him for what they require. Above all, Christ wants us to ask in His name for the courage to be His doers, fellow workers and worshippers with Him in His work.

But asking the Father in Christ's name means more than begging favors. It means praying His prayer, praying as He did all His life. It means asking the Father for grace for all men to know and love Him: praying for sinners, for world conversion, for the sick, the poor, the homeless, the pagans, the persecuted. Christ's promise is startling: *Whatsoever you ask.* We all pray, and some pray a great deal. But perhaps we do not pray Christ's prayer, perhaps we do not pray it well, perhaps we do not pray in His name. On the day when the whole Church with all its members together fulfills this command of Christ our Head, on that day we shall receive, and our joy — and the joy of the world — will be full.

1. Be doers of the word, and not hearers only, deceiving yourselves (Epistle).

2. Blessed be the Lord, Who hath not turned away my prayer, nor His mercy from me (Offertory verse).

3. Sing ye to the Lord, alleluia; sing ye to the Lord, and bless His Name; show forth His salvation from day to day, alleluia, alleluia (Communion verse).

FEAST OF THE ASCENSION

SHOUT UNTO GOD

Today we do not celebrate the mere memory of the Ascension of our Lord, we celebrate the Ascension. "Grant, we implore Thee, O Almighty God, that we who believe Thine only-begotten Son, our Redeemer, to have ascended *this day* into heaven, may also ourselves dwell in spirit amid heavenly things" (Collect). This day our Lord ascends from our midst. And the joy that bursts forth in the variable parts of this Mass is Christ's own joy. "O clap your hands, all ye nations; shout unto God with the voice of joy" (Introit).

The glory of this feast is all Christ's. It is the greatest of the feasts of His exaltation, it is the feast of His coronation as King and Lord of the world. "Glorify the King of Kings and sing a hymn unto God" (Vespers antiphon).

We plunge into the Church's celebration today in order to congratulate our Lord, to thank the Father for what He has done for our Head and our Brother, and to add our small praise to that of all the earth and heaven, too. We try to be obedient to the command of

152

the Church: "Sing ye to the Lord, Who mounteth above the heaven of heavens to the east. Alleluia" (Communion verse).

PARTAKERS OF HIS GODHEAD

What does the Ascension mean to us? To answer that question we must recall one of the fundamental principles of the Church Year, namely, that what is depicted in the variable parts of the Mass becomes reality for us in the sacrifice part. Accordingly, our altar is the Mount of the Ascension. We stand there with the disciples. Our Lord appears to us. He upbraids us for our incredulity and hardness of heart, for our slowness and unwillingness to believe and to become doers of His word and His work, for our hesitation to intensify our union with Him.

Then we see Him rise up into heaven. That is the unforgettable lesson that Christ gives us. All His life He spoke to us by word of mouth. But He teaches best of all by action. Seeing Him going up to heaven we receive a true and exact understanding of ourselves and our life in this world, of our great dignity and our greater destiny.

For the idea of our dignity we can look to the Preface. It tells us that Christ was lifted up into heaven "so that He might make us partakers of his Godhead." He had to ascend to His Father so that He could send us the Spirit of Love who would make us temples of the Divinity.

As for our destiny — it is with Christ, in that true

Home of ours where He is now preparing a place for us. St. Leo the Great writes in today's Second Nocturne lessons: "This day is not only the possession of Paradise made sure unto us; but in the Person of our Head we have actually begun ourselves to enter into the heavenly home." In the Collect we pray God to give us the insight to think of that place always and to dwell there even now in spirit and desire.

EARNING OUR ASCENSION

But the Christian should be no dreamer. It is good for us to be on the Mount of the Ascension, watching our Lord going up into heaven, longing to be with Him in body as well as in spirit. But to us also the Angels say: "Why do you stand looking up to heaven? This Jesus will come again" (Epistle). And Jesus' last words echo in our ears: "Go ye into the whole world and preach the gospel to every creature" (Gospel). This is our commission. Our Lord's last words on earth, expressing His most fervent desire, must be obeyed.

Therefore, back to earth... and to work. Our ascension has to be earned in this world, with this mental and bodily equipment we now have, in this work, this vocation in which God has placed us. The ideal Christian life is to dwell on high and to work below, completing the Redemption our Lord began and which He has now entrusted in our hands, completing it in our fellowmen, but first of all in ourselves. "Mercifully grant, O Lord, that we may be freed from present dangers and finally arrive at everlasting life" (Secret prayer).

There is still much to be done — both in ourselves and in the world. And, if we are to believe the alarmists, time is running out. But the Christian cannot be a pessimist. Christ's Ascension is the guarantee of ours. But we must work, we must not stand around idle. We will not be alone. In nine days we too shall receive power "when the Holy Spirit comes upon us" (Epistle), and we shall be witnesses for Christs in all parts of our land.

> "Thou Guide to heaven, and Thou the Way!
> Be Thou the Goal where our hearts tend;
> Be Thou our Joy 'mid tears, we pray,
> Be Thou our Life's sweet Prize and end"

> (Vespers hymn).

FOOD FOR THE WAY

1. O clap your hands, all ye nations; shout unto God with the voice of joy (Introit).
2. Men of Galilee, why do you stand looking up to heaven? This Jesus will come again (Epistle).
3. God is ascended in jubilee, and the Lord with the sound of trumpet. Alleluia (Offertory verse).

SUNDAY WITHIN THE OCTAVE
OF ASCENSION

I HAVE SOUGHT THY FACE

This Sunday Mass echoes the Ascension: "God is ascended with jubilee; and the Lord with the sound of trumpet" (Offertory verse). But most of all, it prepares for the coming of the Holy Spirit on Pentecost: "But when the Advocate has come, whom I will send you from the Father, the Spirit of truth who proceeds from the Father, he will bear witness concerning me" (Gospel).

The Mass gives a tableau of the thoughts of the apostles that first Sunday within the Octave of the Ascension. They remembered Christ's words: "I will not leave you orphans; but I go away and I am coming to you, and your heart shall rejoice" (Alleluia verse).

But here they are, deprived of His visible presence, missing Him whom they had so loved, and waiting, waiting. The Introit expresses both their ardent love and their homesickness for Christ, as well as their earnest prayer for the coming of the Holy Spirit and the fulfillment of Jesus' promise. "Hear, O Lord, my voice, with which I have cried to Thee: my heart hath said to Thee, I have sought Thy face. Thy face, O Lord, I will seek: turn not Thy face from me... The Lord is my light and my salvation, whom shall I fear?"

And there were other thoughts in their minds, disturbing and terrifying from a human point of view. For they remembered their Master's words: "These things I have spoken to you that you may not be scandalized. They will expel you from the synagogues. Yes, the hour is coming for everyone who kills you to think he is offering worship to God. And these things they will do because they have not known the Father nor me. But these things I have spoken to you, that when the time for them has come you may remember that I told you" (Gospel). We can hardly blame them if they were alarmed, not yet having been "confirmed" by the Holy Spirit. It is not easy to look forward to being killed.

PRUDENT AND WATCHFUL IN PRAYERS

These thoughts of the apostles (except for their worry) should be our thoughts today. We, too, can express our love and longing for Christ in those beautiful Introit words and in today's Collect: "O Almighty and Everlasting God, grant that we may have *a will devoted to Thee* and *a sincere heart to serve Thy Majesty.*" Here we ask for the very same gifts that characterized Christ Himself. A will devoted to God unites us to God so that He can predominate in our lives. A sincere heart ever ready to serve God's Majesty is a heart aflame for the glory of God. We could hardly ask for anything that could give greater impetus and effect to our apostolic work.

Above all, we must look forward with sincere longing for the coming of the Holy Spirit to us next Sunday. Recall how the Holy Spirit on the first Pentecost made these fearful, self-seeking, disunited men into a fearless, bold, God-seeking and God-loving unit. We, too, may be fearful and individualistic. We, too, face misunderstanding and perhaps even persecution if we are true to our apostolic vocation. But the Holy Spirit will come to us and dwell in us and unify us; and Christ's prayer for us will not fail: "Father, while I was with them, I kept them whom Thou gavest me; but now I come to Thee: I pray not that Thou shouldst take them out of the world, but that *Thou shouldst keep them from evil*" (Communion verse). "The Lord is my light and my salvation: whom shall I fear" (Introit)?

Meanwhile, as we wait, we can heed St. Peter's advice: "Beloved: be prudent and watchful in prayers. But above all things have a constant mutual charity among yourselves; for charity covers a multitude of sins. Be hospitable to one another without murmuring... that in all things God may be honored through Jesus Christ our Lord" (Epistle). There can be no better preparation for the coming of the Spirit of Love into our hearts than loving hearts that have been shaped and formed by a practice of daily service of Christ in our neighbor.

FOOD FOR THE WAY

1. My heart hath said to Thee, I have sought Thy face,

Thy face, O Lord, I will seek: turn not away Thy face from me (Introit).

2. I will not leave you orphans; I go away and I am coming to you, and your heart shall rejoice (Alleluia verse).

3. The Lord is my light and my salvation; whom shall I fear (Introit)?

PENTECOST

We have to try to grasp what a stupendous event that first Pentecost was. See the handful of men pressed together around Mary in the Upper Room. Ten days have passed since they beheld their Christ rising up from their midst. Ten days of waiting, ten days of fear behind locked doors, ten days of longing expectation and prayer.

Then the thing happened. The sudden rush of wind with its great swarming noise filling the whole house where they were sitting, the tongues of fire that came to rest on each of their heads. That was the external, the visible. Interiorly their hearts overflowed with joy, peace, love. We do not know how many moments they remained rapt in tender enjoyment of their divine visitation; but certainly it was long enough for them to realize how right our Lord had been when He told them, "It is expedient for you that I depart, for if I do not go, the Advocate will not come to you" (John 16:7). He had been right always, but this time more than ever before.

Then, they moved from contemplation into action, bursting wide the locked doors of their "church." They

160

passed from the celebration of the Liturgy into the apostolate of the word and the work. Timid, backward Galilean fisherman opened their mouths and were miraculously understood each in their own tongue by Parthians, Medes, Cretans, Arabians, who heard, saw, and were converted. And in one hour the New Christ, the Catholic Church, Christ's Mystical Body, numbered some three thousand new cells.

COME, HOLY SPIRIT

More than 1900 Pentecosts have since been celebrated by Christ's Mystical Body, and with each celebration Christ continues to grow and to take possession of the hearts of men. But we should not speak of Pentecosts, but of *Pentecost*, because everything in the Church — her life of glorification of God, her Mass, Sacraments, Liturgical Year, her apostolic activity and prayer life — all this is nothing else than the flowering of that first wonderful Feast. We are living in the Age of the Holy Spirit, Father Daniélou tells us, and when this age is over, Christ will be all and in all.

Today the Church celebrates Pentecost with more than her customary joy and enthusiasm. "Wherefore does the whole world rejoice with exceeding great joy throughout all the earth; and the hosts above, and the angelic powers also join in singing the hymn of Thy glory without ceasing" (Preface). But mingled with her joy is her urgent and poignant prayer for the full effects of the Holy Spirit in her members. "Cleanse our hearts

161

by the light of the Holy Spirit" (Secret prayer). For the Church realizes the great power of the Spirit and the even greater need her world has for the possible results of such a visitation.

"Send forth Thy Spirit, and there will be a fresh creation; Thou wilt re-people the earth: COME, HOLY SPIRIT, fill the hearts of Thy faithful and kindle in them the fire of Thy love" (Alleluia verse, Knox translation).

The Church knows her children better than they know themselves. Although they are chosen by Christ and sealed as His members in Baptism, anointed with His Holy Spirit unto a sharing in His priestly work in Confirmation, she knows how difficult they find it to live up to their vocation. She has her personal experience of their blindness to divine things, of how bored they can become trying to fill the vast spaces of their hearts-made-for-God with the trinket drops of passing sense-pleasures. She knows how afraid they are of being by themselves, alone with their God. She is aware of their mediocrity, their complacency, their luke-warmness — all of which has gone into their failure to win their world for Christ.

And she knows her world, too: its futility, its bore-dom, its wars, its idolatry of false gods, its consequent fear and despair. With all this in mind, the Church prays: "May the outpouring of the Holy Spirit purify our hearts, O Lord, and so sprinkle them with the dew of His interior grace that they may be fruitful in good works" (Postcommunion prayer).

THE RIGHT KIND OF INEBRIATION

The Holy Spirit is Divine Light, dispelling the darkness of ever-present paganism. He brings treasures that endure. He is consolation in pain. He brings peace and solace. He heals wounds, renews strength, freshens the dryness of our spirits, bends rigid wills, fills frozen hearts with fervor (Sequence). Come, fill our hearts!

They said that the apostles were inebriated; and in a way they were, in spite of St. Peter's protestations that it was only nine o'clock in the morning (Read the Acts of the Apostles, Chapter two). But the inebriating drink in this case was not wine, but a new kind of Spirit, distilled in the heart of God.

We, too, may drink our fill of this Spirit today. The Christian who is truly filled with the Holy Spirit is *fearless*, for he knows Who is in him. He is full of love and goodness towards others; and since *love* and *goodness* spread like fire, he wants everyone else to share his joy in their possession. Finally, he is *enthusiastic* about God and Christ and the Church and does everything in his power to bring others to share in his enthusiam.

We, the Church, and our world can stand a lot of this kind of inebriation. It is the basis of the apostolate.

FOOD FOR THE WAY

1. The Spirit of the Lord hath filled the whole earth, alleluia (Introit)!

163

2. If anyone love me, he will keep my word, and my Father will love him, and we will come to him and make our abode with him (Gospel).

3. Come, O Holy Spirit, fill the hearts of Thy faithful: and kindle in them the fire of Thy love (Alleluia verse).

TRINITY SUNDAY

GIVING THE TRINITY ITS DUE

That there are three divine Persons in one God is the deepest mystery our Lord revealed. We shall never grasp it fully either in this life or in the next. When human, limited minds try to fathom infinite truth, they must necessarily be satisfied with glimpses and flashes of understanding — glimpses that increase in proportion to our constant study, effort, and prayer.

But if we cannot understand the Trinity, if we tire of study, we can always praise and adore. Which is exactly what this Feast helps us to do. This Mass is a grand *Te Deum*, an extended *Gloria* to the Blessed Trinity, bursting forth from a grateful people "because He has shown His mercy to us" (Offertory verse).

We are grateful and praiseful because of what the Blessed Trinity has done for us. Recall the events of the past half year: the Father so loved us that He sent His Son to become one of us, to suffer and die for us. The Son so loved us that He sent the Holy Spirit to become the Life of our individual souls and the life principle of the whole Mystical Body. "O the depth of the riches of the wisdom and of the knowledge of God! How incomprehensible are his judgments and how unsearchable are his ways... For from him and through him and unto him are all things. To him be the glory forever, amen" (Epistle).

We are also, and perhaps above all, grateful because the Blessed Trinity is the Blessed Trinity, because God is God, because He is the totality of love, of life, of goodness, of beauty. "O Lord our Lord, how wonderful is Thy Name in all the earth" (Introit). We praise Thee, we bless Thee, we adore Thee, we glorify Thee, we give Thee thanks for Thy great glory.

FREE ADORATION

This feast helps us to realize that we are most faithful to our vocation as members of Christ's Mystical Body when our life is dominated by the spirit of praise of God and of burning zeal for His glory. It has so often been said that the stars, the wonderful forces of nature, the mountains, streams and plants, the unthinking animals of the earth and seas — all glorify and praise the Blessed Trinity just by being what they are and by blindly following nature's laws. But they cannot know the result of their adoration, they cannot be improved by it.

We, on the other hand, by our praise and because of it, can advance in perfection and in union with God steadily and surely. For we are human, we are made in the likeness of God Himself, we have minds, wills, emotions, as well as bodies. We are sons and daughters of a loving Father who desires us to make free and responsible use of the gifts He has given us.

God wants our praise and adoration — not for His own sake (He is not like an imperial potentate who could be flattered by our bowings and kneelings) — but because it is only through our praise and adoration that He can find an entrance into our beings, there to work His transforming, unifying wonders within us. Praise and adoration are our response as human beings to God as the Supreme Value of life, a response that inevitably calls forth from Him a beneficent and loving reply. Father Pierre Charles says: "Exterior praise has no meaning unless it is the expression of total surrender to an invading God." Therefore, "Blessed be God the Father, and the only-begotten Son of God, and also the Holy Spirit; because He hath shown His mercy toward us" (Offertory verse).

PRAISE AND APOSTOLATE

The spirit of praise, therefore, works heavenward and earthward: it opens up our eyes to vistas of the heart and mystery of God; and it opens up the way for God into our hearts and beings. But there are endless possibilities in the spirit of praise, the beautiful daughter of this blessed Trinity feast. Father Daniélou, in his book *The Salvation of the Nations*, points out how the spirit of praise is the key to the apostolate.

Here is how he explains it: the more we praise God, the better we will come to know Him — His greatness and His excellence — and the more we will appreciate and admire His goodness. The more, too, we will want to please Him. This is the way it was with Christ. All

167

His life He sought His Father's glory and only that. So with all the saints.

This desire to please God (who is Love) will have a threefold effect on us: first of all, it will make us aware of our own unworthiness in His presence, and will make us desire and strive for self-purification. Secondly, it will make us yearn for greater union with Him (who is Life). And thirdly it will *make us want to bring souls to Him.* We will be struck by the scandal that He who is Love, He who is Life of souls, He who is boundless Goodness, is not loved and served and desired by all men. This conviction is the source and soul of the apostolate.

"Blessed art Thou, O Lord, Who beholdest the depths, and sittest upon the cherubim. Blessed art Thou, O Lord, in the firmament of heaven, and worthy of praise forever. Blessed art Thou, O Lord God of our fathers, and worthy of praise forever" (Gradual). Our God is worthy of praise and love. We must procure it for Him.

The purpose of the Sundays after Pentecost is the unfolding within us of the divine Life we received in our celebration of Lent, Easter, Pentecost. This growth depends mostly on God's mercy. But we can release that divine mercy by developing the attitude towards God that this Mass holds out to us and by making that attitude habitual. "We pray Thee, O Lord, our God, to sanctify the victim of our offering and, as a result of it, *make of us an eternal offering to Thee*" (Secret prayer). When we learn to make of our daily life a constant offering of praise to our God, then we will truly be His beloved sons, His apostles. For then we will have the mind of Christ who was able to say: "Father, I have glorified thee on earth; I have accomplished the work that thou hast given me to do" (John 17:4).

FOOD FOR THE WAY

1. O Lord, our Lord, how wonderful is Thy Name in all the earth (Introit).
2. From him and through him and unto him are all things. To him be the glory forever (Epistle).
3. Behold, I am with you all days, even unto the consummation of the world (Gospel).

FEAST OF CORPUS CHRISTI

MEAT IN DUE SEASON

"One reason why we must pray and meditate," says Father Martindale, "is that spiritual things are veiled and invisible to the eye, and unless we keep the mind occupied with them they become unreal to us." There is special danger of a sense of unreality creeping over and dulling our appreciation of the Eucharist. We sometimes become too used to it, we take it too much for granted. We need constant meditation and reflection on its glories; and above all, we need a great feast like Corpus Christi, with its procession, its hymns, its joyous decorations, to break the crust that habit and routine too often form over the deep appreciation of the Mass and holy Communion that we should have.

This feast takes us into the deep depths of the heart of man and shows us how very much that heart requires the Eucharist. "The eyes of all hope in Thee, O Lord, and Thou givest them meat in due season. Thou openest Thy hand, and fillest every living creature with blessing" (Gradual).

Only the God Who made the human heart knows fully the food that can satisfy it. He knows that, to be truly filled, man needs more than the empty shells of half truths and the frilly salads of amusement and escapism that are offered in theatres, restaurants, ballrooms, and even libraries. Man needs the "fat of wheat and the honey from the rock" (Introit) of divine Life, Truth, Love. And God wonderfully provides for all those human needs in the Blessed Eucharist.

"O Sacred Banquet, in which Christ is received;
The memory of His passion is renewed;
The mind is filled with grace ;
And a pledge of future glory is given to us
(Magnificat antiphon).

PROCLAIMING THE LORD'S DEATH

The Feast also takes us to the source of the Eucharist. "The Lord Jesus, on the night in which He was betrayed, took bread, and giving thanks, broke, and said: 'Take and eat. THIS IS MY BODY WHICH SHALL BE GIVEN FOR YOU. Do this in remembrance of me.' In like manner also the cup, after he had supped, saying, 'THIS CUP IS THE NEW COVENANT IN MY BLOOD; do this as often as you drink it, in remembrance of me. FOR AS OFTEN AS YOU SHALL EAT THIS BREAD AND DRINK THE CUP, YOU PROCLAIM THE DEATH OF THE LORD, UNTIL HE COMES" (Epistle).

Therefore, the Eucharist is Christ's sacrifice of Himself, His passion and death, re-enacted in our midst. It is the proclaiming of His death. If we ever fully grasped

171

that fact, there would not be enough churches in the world, there would be no pagans, no heretics or schismatics; there would only be saints. Through the hands of His Church, the Son of God offers Himself to the Father. "Through Him, and with Him, and in Him, is to Thee, God the Father Almighty, in the unity of the Holy Spirit, ALL HONOR AND GLORY" (Canon).

Thus does the sacrifice part of the Mass end. The answers of the people to that splendid doxology is simple, but tremendously effective *and important.* "Amen," we say. "So be it." We here give our consent to the whole wonderful, glorious, glorifying, worshipful work of Christ our Lord. All honor and glory be to our God through Christ our Head. AMEN.

VICTIMS ALL

We have been thinking and talking about praise and adoration as being absolutely essential to our life as men and as apostles. The Mass is the fullness, the summit, of praise, adoration, and glorification, that can possibly be offered to God. And we can join ourselves to it, give our free consent to it, in a way make it our own. SO BE IT.

We saw last week that it is through our praise that we can open up the way of the invading God into our lives. If just a plain sincere GLORY BE TO THE FATHER, AND TO THE SON, AND TO THE HOLY GHOST opens up our souls to God, what must be the invitation that results from Christ's and our praise at holy Mass! Only God could have conceived the answer He holds out to us: "Take and eat. This is my body WHICH SHALL BE GIVEN FOR YOU... This cup is the new covenant in my blood." "My flesh is food indeed, and my blood is drink indeed. He who eats my flesh, and drinks my blood, abides in me and I in him... This is the bread that has come down from heaven; not as your fathers ate the manna and died. He who eats this bread shall live forever" (Gospel).

God answers our praise by giving us His Son to be our food. But this is *sacrificial food*, it is partaking of the Divine Victim, the Lamb of God. It is He, Christ, — adoring, glorifying, praising the Father and loving, pitiying, unifying mankind — who invades our life and wishes to take over in it.

"The mind is filled with grace; and a pledge of future glory is given to us." The grace will be ours... and the guarantee of eternal glory. But not without our free cooperation with the spirit of the Victim Christ, not without our own lives being sacrificial, not without our also becoming victims with Christ to the glory of God and the sanctification of souls. That has been said before. It can never be too often repeated. It is exactly what we pray for today: "Grant us, we beseech Thee, so to reverence the sacred mysteries of Thy Body and Blood, that we may ever experience within us the fruit of Thy Redemption" (Collect). The fruit of the Redemption is none other than the grace of being Christ-like in all our thoughts, words, and deeds. If we do that, we will be true apostles. And then God's answer to our Postcommunion prayer will fill us with joy overflowing: "Grant us, we beseech Thee, O Lord, to be filled with the eternal enjoyment of Thy Divinity, which is prefigured here in this life by the reception of Thy precious Body and Blood."

> Jesu! Shepherd of the sheep!
> Thou Thy flock in safety keep.
> Living bread! Thy life supply;
> Strengthen us, or else we die:
> Fill us with celestial grace. (Sequence).

FOOD FOR THE WAY

1. Rejoice to God our helper; sing aloud to the God of Jacob (Introit)!
2. The eyes of all hope in Thee, O Lord, and Thou givest them meat in due season (Gradual).
3. Whoever eats this bread or drinks the cup of the Lord unworthily, will be guilty of the Body and Blood of the Lord (Communion verse).

SUNDAY WITHIN THE OCTAVE
OF CORPUS CHRISTI

THE GREAT BANQUET

This Sunday's Mass was composed centuries before the Feast of Corpus Christi; but those who put it together must have possessed a prophetic sense; for its texts fit in perfectly with the spirit of the great feast of the Blessed Sacrament.

As in so many Sunday Masses, the Gospel dominates the other texts. It is our Lord's parable about the "man who made a great supper and invited many," only to have most of his guests turn him down — in each case with the flimsiest of excuses, excuses quite as foolish as the ones that we modern Catholics think up for avoiding frequent Communion. The man finally had to go out into the highways and hedges to compel the wayfarers to come in so that his banquet hall would be filled. "But I say to you, that none of these men that were invited shall taste of my supper" (Gospel).

Under the veil of this parable, our Lord is obviously speaking of the redemption which He offered to the human race. He came into His own, but His own refused to accept Him. The Pharisees and leaders of the Chosen People would have nothing to do with a Savior who would not cater to their dreams of national political advancement. He was hardly more successful with the lesser citizens of the town and countryside; therefore, He had to go to the gentiles and pagans. That is where we all fit in. We can say in full truth: "The Lord became my Protector, and He brought me forth into a large place: *He saved me*, because He was well pleased with me" (Introit).

However, we can also apply the parable to the Blessed Eucharist, God's own Banquet, to which He invites so many and from which people stay away in such large numbers. God so insists on our partaking of the Banquet because He knows as we cannot know how utterly necessary the Banquet is for us. There is simply no good excuse for staying away. Nor is there any excuse for not eating to the full of this strong Food of eternal life. There can be no dieting here, no nibbling. "Unless you eat the flesh of the Son of Man, and drink his blood, you shall not have life in you" (John 6:54).

WE HAVE KNOWN THE CHARITY OF GOD

But there is something in the Mass for those of us who do eat frequently and daily at the Banquet. In the Epistle St. John speaks of charity: "We know that we have passed from death to life, because we love the brethren. He who does not love abides in death. Everyone who hates his brother is a murderer... In this we have come to know his love, that he laid down his life

176

for us; and we likewise ought to lay down our life for the brethren."

We know from our own experience that holy Communion does us little good if our hearts are filled with suspicion, hatred, greed, and avarice. Therefore, let us not love God and our neighbor in word or in tongue, but in deed and in truth. Sharing in Mass and Communion with hearts on fire with love will make us come away with more love. He laid down His life for us: we must lay down our life for the brethren. And in laying down our lives for them, in giving ourselves to them, they will come to realize what they are missing in their constant rejection of His invitation to come themselves to the Banquet hall.

Another result of frequent participation in the Sacrifice of the Mass and Communion, the fruit of the Sacrifice, must be the rooting out of sin and the corresponding perfecting of our lives. "May this offering, O Lord, about to be dedicated to Thy holy Name, *purify us and make us advance day by day in the practice of a heavenly life*" (Secret prayer). But we shall be purified and shall advance in the practice of a heavenly life only on condition that we allow the sacrificial, love-inspired mind of Christ the Victim to replace our self-loving, ease-concerned attitudes towards God and our fellowmen.

FEAR AND LOVE

The Eucharist, then, is the mainspring of Christian, apostolic living. God would not be so insistent on our partaking of it if it were optional, if we and our world

177

could just as well do without it. One of the best gifts it provides for us is the answer to today's Collect in which we pray for "perpertual fear and love of Thy holy Name," which means fear and love for God Himself. There is something seriously wanting in an attitude towards God that is not based on fear (reverence) and love. The best place for training ourselves in the true Christian attitude towards God is the Holy Sacrifice itself; for the Mass, with its prayer and sacred action is the world's greatest testimony to the awesome sovereignty and supremacy of God. It re-enacts Christ's sacrifice on Calvary at which the angels veil their faces in reverence and wonder! Holy, holy, holy, Lord God of Hosts! Heaven and earth are filled with Thy glory!

Our daily plunging into the spirit of the Confiteor, Kyrie, Gloria, Sanctus, and Doxology at the end of the Canon, cannot but imprint in our minds and hearts the sense of reverential fear that God's majesty demands of us. But God is not only the supreme Lord, as Cardinal Suhard points out, He is also Emmanuel, God-with-us. And where is He more with us than in Holy Communion wherein He becomes our Food?

The Eucharist, Sacrifice and Communion, is training for the apostolate and training for heaven. Even though we are still in the world, we are redeemed, for He has chosen us (Introit). We may grieve a little, but "In our trouble we cry to the Lord, and He hears us and delivers our soul from wicked eyes and a deceitful tongue" (Gradual).

What must be our reaction to the blessed invitation that He gives to us? "I will love Thee, O Lord my strength: the Lord is my firmament, and my refuge, and

178

my deliverer" (Introit). We offer Him in Sacrifice and ourselves with Him. He gives us Himself. Therefore, "I will sing to the Lord, Who giveth me good things: and I will sing to the Name of the Lord most high" (Communion verse). But St. John has the last word: "My dear children, let us not love in word, neither with the tongue, but in deed and in truth" (Epistle). Our love, our gratitude will be sincere and honest in deed and in truth only if it overflows into the apostolate of the streets and factories of the city, the highways and hedges, the town and farms, spending ourselves so that His house may be filled.

FOOD FOR THE WAY

1. I will love Thee, O Lord my strength: the Lord is my firmament, and my refuge, and my deliverer (Introit).
2. Turn to me, O Lord, and deliver my soul: O save me for Thy mercy's sake (Offertory verse).
3. I will sing to the Lord, Who giveth me good things (Communion verse).

THIRD SUNDAY AFTER PENTECOST

JOY IN HEAVEN

The Son of God became man in order to seek out and rescue sinners and to become their Way, their Truth, their Life. He lived among sinners, preached to them, suffered and died for them. In today's Gospel our Lord's enemies, the Pharisees, describe His life, character and work in a phrase that is as beautiful as it is all-embracing and exact: "This man welcomes sinners and eats with them." Everything He did, He did for sinners. Because He loved them. But most of all because He loved His Father and knew that He could best prove His love for His Father by rescuing sinners and bringing them back to His and their heavenly Father as trophies of love.

"There will be joy in heaven over one sinner who repents, more than over ninety-nine just who have no need of repentance" (Gospel). Jesus is the Good Shepherd who goes out after the sheep who is lost, finds it, and lays it on His shoulders rejoicing. He did that all during His earthly life. "I am the good shepherd," He said to us on the Second Sunday after Easter. "The good shepherd lays down his life for his sheep."

180

But the best proof of His being a Good Shepherd and a friend of sinners is that He founded His Church to continue His work. It is above all in His Church that the Pharisees' characterization of Christ is fulfilled. For it is in the Church that He truly welcomes sinners and eats with them at the Eucharistic table. It is in the Church that He re-enacts His historical life so as to allow all of us, saints and sinners, to follow and share in it. And all this adds up to one thing: Christ's undying, persistent, infinite love for us.

During the past half year, we have seen with our own eyes and followed with our ears and hearts the unfolding of His love. Last Friday the Church brought that divine love for us, sinners all, to a wonderful focus in the celebration of the Feast of the Sacred Heart. And today, with her Gospel of the Good Shepherd, she overwhelms us with that idea. The Heart of Christ pierced with a soldier's lance — the Good Shepherd seeking out that which was lost : these two symbols cry out to us Christ's dedication to the will of His Father and His love for us. We must never allow ourselves to forget them.

DANGEROUS PASTURES

But unfortunately we do forget and have forgotten; and this is the way we sound: "Look upon me, O Lord, and have mercy on me; for I am alone and poor. See my abjection and labor; and forgive me all my sins" (Introit). It is such a short while since the great feasts of Easter and Pentecost — feasts that lifted us up to peaks of joy and union with Christ our Shepherd. What has happened to us?

Nothing has happened except that we have strayed from our Shepherd. We are not angels, but human beings. We still live in the world. We are still the prey of temptation and sin. And then there is the devil, depicting for us green pastures of alluring delights and pouncing on us like a roaring lion (Epistle). If we are alone and poor and afraid, it is mostly because we have chosen to separate ourselves from our Good Shepherd and from our fellow members in His flock.

Apart from Him "nothing is strong, nothing is holy" (Collect). Without Him as Guide and chosen Protector, we stray inevitably into those dangerous pastures of "the good things of the present" (Collect), and, instead of using these things with detachment and renunciation, we misuse them, make them ends instead of means, and they ruin us. They make us forget Christ. They blind us to our true purpose in life — union with Him — and when we lose sight of that purpose, we lose all and are alone and poor. There is a famine of the soul that is as painful and distressing as hunger of the body. We cannot live without mental prayer, without a consciously cultivated sense of God's presence in, and influence on, our lives.

CAST THY CARE

But our Shepherd and His Church are still on the job. That is why we are at Mass this morning. We cannot ever stray too far if we live with their map in our hands, the missal, for they are the original guides and protectors leading us along the highways of life to our God. "To Thee, O Lord, have I lifted up my soul: in Thee, my God, I put my trust" (Introit). Thus does the Church make us pray, bringing us back unto the highway to the sheepfold with the very words with which we began our Godward journey last Advent.

Then in the Epistle, she gives us further directions, recalling certain facts of life and travel to us that we may have forgotten in the summer heat of life: "Humble yourselves under the mighty hand of God, that He may exalt you in the time of visitation; *cast all your anxiety upon him, because he cares for you.* Be sober, be watchful... But the God of all grace, who has called us unto his eternal glory in Christ Jesus, will himself, after we have suffered a little while, perfect, strengthen and establish us."

Therefore, we are to expect the heat of temptation, worry, the feeling of being abandoned by our Shepherd. Our forgetfulness of God and our neglect of prayer have deserved all this and more. We are to expect the cross and suffering so that we may learn of Him because He is meek and humble of heart. We must not allow ourselves to be overwhelmed by the world's fear and pessimistic despair. His grace is sufficient for us. "This man welcomes sinners and eats with them." He loves us. All we have to do is to "cast our care upon Him and He shall sustain us." (Gradual).

1. To Thee, O Lord, have I lifted up my soul: in Thee, my God, I put my trust; let me not be ashamed (Introit).

2. Thou hast not forsaken them that seek Thee: sing ye to the Lord, Who dwelleth in Sion: for He hath not forgotten the cry of the poor (Offertory verse).

3. I say to you, there will be joy among the angels of God over one sinner who repents (Communion verse).

FOURTH SUNDAY AFTER PENTECOST

SIMON PETER'S SHIP

"And getting into one of the ships, the one that was Simon's, he besought him to put out a little from the land. And sitting down, he began to teach the crowds from the boat" (Gospel).

The ship that was Simon Peter's is changed in appearance since the day it was first launched. The small fishing boat of Lake Genesareth is now a great liner, sailing the oceans of the world. But it is still Peter's ship. Peter's ship is the Catholic Church, and its Captain is the same Christ who went up into it then and who promised that He would be with it all days, even to the end of the world.

We who are baptized make up the crew and passenger list of the ship. We are on a voyage, the voyage of our life in the world. It is not a pleasure cruise, but a pilgrimage, and the waters we sail are dangerous — full of hidden rocks and enemy submarines, ready at any moment to attack and try to sink us. Moreover, within the ship itself, among us who are the crew and passengers, our own sinful weakness flares up in occasional mutiny against our Captain's directions and way of life. Hence, our Secret prayer today: "In Thy mercy compel our rebellious wills to turn unto Thee."

We tend to forget (especially when the enemy attacks with his most insidious and insistent temptations) that our ship is absolutely safe — as long as we remain in it and as long as we keep up confidence in our Captain. "Why are you fearful?" He says to us, "It is I, fear not." Instead of fearing, we should say: "The Lord is my light and my salvation: whom shall I fear? The Lord is the protector of my life: of whom shall I be afraid? My enemies that trouble me have themselves been weakened and have fallen" (Introit).

DON'T GIVE UP THE SHIP

Without Christ our Captain, and His visible representative, our Holy Father, we would have reason to be afraid. Without Christ, we would long ago have perished and become victims of the combined efforts of our own mutiny, temptations from within and without, and starvation. But Christ keeps up our morale, if we only stay close to Him as He unerringly steers our Ship towards its eternal goal.

With Him we pray: "Help us, O God, our Savior; and for the honor of Thy name, deliver us" (Gradual). He never fails to answer that prayer, especially when — like the crowds on the shore of Lake Genesareth — we press together around Him and with one voice plead with faith and confidence that we shall be heard. "And sitting down, He began to teach the crowds from the ship." His answer to our prayer is His *teaching* and His *nourishment*, each of which He holds out to us in abundance at morning Mass.

Every day (or every week, if duties at our particular post keep us from being there more often) He gathers us together, and at His word we let down the nets of our hearts into the ocean of our faith, and He invariably fills them, rejoicing us with the abundance and size of our catch.

He fills our nets with *Himself*. (One of the early Christian symbols for Christ was that of a fish. It came about in this way: the Greek word for fish, IKTUS, is made up of the first letters of the words JESUS CHRIST, GOD'S SON, SAVIOR). And when our nets are filled with Christ, we have reason to cry out: "The Lord is my firmament, and my refuge, and my deliverer; my God is my helper" (Communion verse).

With the light of our Captain guiding us, we can see with His eyes. We can see through to the end of the voyage when it shall be revealed to us that "the sufferings of the present time are not worthy to be compared with the glory to come that will be revealed in us" (Epistle). Therefore, the message of today's Mass is: DON'T GIVE UP THE SHIP! We are to do our work well in the particular shipboard task our Captain has given us, our vocation, eat our fill at daily Mass, have confidence in and love for our Captain and for one another. He, Christ, will take care of the rest: the guiding, the protecting, the safe landings. He will "enlighten our eyes, that we never sleep in death; lest at any time our enemy say: I have prevailed against them" (Offertory verse).

One of our temptations, as passengers on Christ's ship, is to feel over-satisfied with being aboard and unconcerned about taking on other passengers. We too easily forget our Lord's desire for a full ship — loaded with passengers. Or, if we have been active in trying to bring others into the ship with us, there is danger of being discouraged at lack of results. "Master, the whole night through we have toiled and have taken nothing" (Gospel).

It has been mentioned before in these pages, but it bears repeating: our work in the apostolate is Christ's work, done in His name and at His command: "Launch out into the deep; lower your nets for a catch... *Do not be afraid*; henceforth, thou shalt catch men." As long as we look on the apostolate as our work exclusively, rather than Christ's, we shall labor the whole voyage through, catching nothing. We must trust in Christ, fear no empty nets, leave the results in His hands. Our constant attitude must be that of Peter: "At thy word I will lower the net."

"May the Sacrament we have received purify us, we beseech Thee, O Lord, and may its gift defend us" (Postcommunion prayer). May it purify us of self-love, sloth, and lack of trust. And above all, may it defend us against the thought that Christ has no need of our efforts, small though they may seem to us!

FOOD FOR THE WAY

1. O God, Who sittest upon the throne, and judgest justice, be Thou the refuge of the poor in tribulation (Alleluia verse).
2. And when they had brought their boats to land, they left all and followed Him (Gospel).
3. The Lord is my firmament, and my refuge, and my deliverer; my God is my helper (Communion verse).

FIFTH SUNDAY AFTER PENTECOST

BE ALL LIKE-MINDED

To understand today's Mass we have to recall what we are as Christians. St. Paul uses the human body to illustrate the great truth of our oneness with one another and with Christ. The human body is made up of a head and a multitude of members, internal and external, all important, and all united into a living unity by a single life-principle, the human soul.

"For as the body is one and has many members, and all the members of the body, many as they are, form one body, so also is it with Christ. For in one Spirit we were all baptized into one body... Now YOU ARE THE BODY OF CHRIST, member for member" (1 Corinthians 12:12, 27).

In the Mystical Body, the Catholic Church, Christ is the Head, we are the members, and the Holy Spirit is the life principle uniting us all together. The same Holy Spirit who is in Christ is in us the members, making us one with Christ, but also one with one another.

Today's Mass is a practical exhortation to all of us to live according to our basic nature as members of the

Christian Community, Christ's Mystical Body. Since we are so closely one by our nature, St. Peter tells us in today's Epistle to start thinking and acting out of a conviction of our oneness. "Be all like-minded in prayer, compassionate, lovers of the brethren, merciful, reserved; humble, not rendering evil for evil, or abuse for abuse, but contrariwise, blessing; for unto this were you called that you might inherit a blessing."

FIRST BE RECONCILED

That is the way it should be, but it must be pointed out that, not only do we refuse to see ourselves as a community, we even give in to divisive practices of thought, word, and deed: to envy, hatred, anger, irritability, sarcasm, grudges. If the Church does not make a greater impact on our world, it is perhaps because we its members no longer pray, live, or act as a community.

The one all-penetrating thought we must have about our neighbor is that God loves our neighbor, that Christ died for our neighbor as He did for us, that He made love of neighbor the *only* sign of the Christian. "By this will all men know that you are my disciples, if you have love for one another" (John 13:35).

It has been said that if we are not at peace with our neighbor, if we are inclined to give in to temptations of hatred, suspicion, and dislike, if we are negligent about thinking in terms of community, our relations with God will be uncertain and unnatural. And our religion will be false, untrue, even hypocritical. Our Lord insists on this in today's Gospel: "Therefore, if thou art offering thy gift at the altar, and there rememberest that thy brother has anything against thee, leave thy gift before the altar and go first to be reconciled to thy brother, and then come and offer thy gift." In other words, *God wants charity among members of the community more than the sacrifices of the various individual components of the community.* Uncharitableness is like a blanket that prevents the sweet incense of *our* worship from rising up as a pleasing odor in the sight of our heavenly Father.

SOURCE OF CHARITY

At the Last Supper our Lord prayed: "That they may be one, even as we are one: I in them and thou in me; that they may be perfected in unity, and that the world may know that thou has sent me" (John 17:23). Christ's prayer must be answered; it will be answered with a little cooperation on our part — cooperation in praying these Sunday Masses together and then living according to the spirit of oneness in that prayer, which means community living in the full sense of the word.

If we are not one with one another, we cannot be one with God. But we can turn that around and say that the main reason why we are not one with one another is that we do not know God well enough, do not love Him as He deserves to be loved. The Church knows this and therefore has us pray today for "the fervor of affection towards Thee, so that by loving Thee in all things and above all things we may obtain thy promises, which exceed all desire" (Collect, Knox translation).

Christ's promise, exceeding all desire, is for unity among His own. By this unity men will know that the Father sent Him. By this unity we will be saved ourselves, by it we will help to save others. "Receive kindly these offerings of Thy servants... that what they have each offered for the glory of Thy name may be of profit *to the salvation of all*" (Secret prayer).

St. Peter, at the end of the Epistle, sums up everything in one shining phrase: ENTHRONE CHRIST AS LORD IN YOUR HEARTS (Knox translation). Having Christ as Lord in our hearts will make us love God with Christ's love, will make us love what Christ loves, make us do what He wants done. It will make us throw our whole being into His Church's community prayer, blessing the Lord who gives us understanding, and setting God always in our sight (Offertory verse). It will help us to see our neighbor with His eyes of merciful love and will compel us to do everything in our power by prayer and action to draw others into His and our Community. Enthroning Christ as Lord in our hearts is the surest way to the fulfillment of today's Communion verse: "One thing I have asked of the Lord, this will I seek after: that I may dwell in the house of the Lord all the days of my life."

FOOD FOR THE WAY

1. Be Thou my helper, forsake me not, nor do Thou despise me, O God my Savior. The Lord is my light, and my salvation: whom shall I fear (Introit)?
2. O Lord God of hosts, give ear to the prayers of Thy servants (Gradual).
3. I will bless the Lord, Who hath given me understanding: I set God always in my sight; for He is at my right hand, that I be not moved (Offertory verse).

SIXTH SUNDAY AFTER PENTECOST

COMPASSION ON THE CROWD

We have once before referred to a favorite theme of Father Parsch to the effect that the sacrifice part of the Mass re-enacts what is depicted in the Gospel of that Mass. This is certainly true today. Our Gospel tells of one of the miraculous multiplications whereby our Lord fed four thousand with seven loaves and a few little fishes. "I have compassion on the crowd, for behold, they have now been with me three days, and have nothing to eat; and if I send them away to their homes fasting, they will faint on the way, for some of them have come from a distance."

We know the chain of circumstances which followed that multiplication. At the Last Supper He changed bread into His Body and wine into His Blood. "Take and eat... THIS IS MY BODY... THIS CUP IS THE NEW COVENANT IN MY BLOOD. DO THIS IN REMEMBRANCE OF ME" (Luke 22:19-20). And we are at Mass today because His apostles and their successors obeyed Christ's command to do what He had done: change bread into His Body and wine into His Blood.

Today we gather in our churches around Jesus in great crowds. Why should He feel differently toward us than He felt toward the Galilean? If He felt compassion for them, He must feel it all the more for us; for we are His people in a stricter sense than they were. We are members of His Mystical Body. He is our Head. We come to Him today with these words on our lips (may they also spring from grateful hearts!): "The Lord is the strength of His people and the protector of the salvation of His anointed: save, O Lord, Thy people, and bless Thy inheritance, and rule them for ever" (Introit).

BAPTIZED INTO CHRIST JESUS

We claim no empty titles. We are Christ's people, His inheritance, His anointed ones, because He made us that way in Baptism. He chose us. He first loved us. The Epistle gives the whole glorious story of how it happened: "Brethren: all we who have been baptized into Christ Jesus have been baptized into His death. For we were buried with him by means of baptism into death, in order that, just as Christ has arisen from the dead through the glory of the Father, so we also may walk in newness of life." But we must read the whole Epistle, meditate on it carefully, and from it we will remember these ideas:

First, that Baptism *makes us die with Christ.* St. Thomas says: "Sinful man is buried by baptism in the

195

passion and death of Christ: it is as if he himself suffered and died with the sufferings and death of the Savior." As a result of our dying with Christ, all sin is destroyed. We can, of course, sin after Baptism, as we know from sad experience. But being one with Christ, sin is unnatural for us, contrary to our new nature. And being one with Him, He helps us to ward it off.

Second, Baptism is death that brings Life, divine Life, to us. *God begins to live in us.* As new branches grafted into a tree live on the sap of the tree, so we are grafted into Christ, to live henceforth on the Life that is in Him. "I am the Vine (the trunk), you are the branches. Abide in me, and I in you" (John 15:5). Because of Baptism He says that to each of us; therefore we are all His members, His people.

Third, this dying to sin so as to have God living in us is to continue all our lives. Our life as Christians is simply our Baptism lived out. When we resist our animal desires, when we seek to overcome all those faults that afflict us, we clear the way to Christ who wishes to take over more and more in our lives. This negative rooting out of defects, together with positive love for Jesus and entering into His life of praise, is our Baptism reaching completion and happy fulfillment in us.

BAPTISM AND EUCHARIST

Because of our Baptism we can pray: "Thou hast been our refuge from generation to generation. In Thee, O Lord, have I hoped, let me never be confounded: deliver me in Thy justice, and release me: bow down

Thy ear to me, make haste to deliver me" (Gradual and Alleluia verses).

But what would Baptism be without Eucharist? What would be the good of Life without the means of nourishing that Life? We are alive physically because we ate material food yesterday and the day before. Physical starvation brings on death. But the new Life we received from Christ in Baptism (or in the Sacrament of Penance if it was lost through mortal sin) needs nourishment just as much as our physical life. As a father and mother have the duty of caring for the child they bring into the world, feeding and sheltering him, so does Christ look after us. "I have compassion on the crowd... Take and eat: THIS IS MY BODY. Take and drink ye all of this, THIS IS THE CHALICE OF MY BLOOD."

He has compassion on us. He gives us new Life, feeds us with Himself, takes us into His holy Community and backs up our prayer with His own authority. But the more experience we have with life and with our own weakness, the more we realize how totally our life and being and progress are in His hands. "Without me you can do nothing" (John 15:5). And the more, too, we realize that we can never pray enough for His help, and that even the will to die to sin and to live unto Him must come from Him. Once we have that conviction of our insufficiency, we can pray with all sincerity the Collect of today's Mass: "O God of all power and might, Thou who art the source of everything that is best, implant in our hearts the love of Thy Name, and grant us an increase of religion, promoting such things as are

197

good, and by Thy watchful care, guarding what Thou hast promoted."

Truly, our God has compassion on us. He "shows forth His wonderful mercies on us, He saves us who trust in Him" (Offertory verse). If we want to know what we can do in return, His Church tells us in the Communion verse: "Offer up in His tabernacle a sacrifice of jubilation; sing and recite a psalm to the Lord." We can offer up a sacrifice of jubilation. But the best return we can make to God is to have compassion on all our neighbors and companions. By our love for them we continue the love and compassion of Christ.

FOOD FOR THE WAY

1. Unto Thee will I cry, O Lord: O my God, be not Thou silent to me (Introit).
2. Thus do you consider yourselves also as dead to sin, but alive to God in Christ Jesus our Lord (Epistle).
3. Perfect Thou my goings in Thy paths, that my footsteps be not moved: incline Thy ear, and hear my words: show forth Thy wonderful mercies, Thou who savest them that trust in Thee, O Lord (Offertory verse).

SEVENTH SUNDAY AFTER PENTECOST

FRUIT UNTO SANCTIFICATION

"Clap your hands, all ye nations: shout unto God with the voice of joy" (Introit). Why, we may wonder, does Mother Church seem so excited today. She herself gives us a hint: "Come, children, harken to me; I will teach you the fear of the Lord. Come ye to Him and be enlightened; and your faces shall not be confounded" (Gradual).

The process of our enlightenment will reveal good cause for excitement, gladness, and joy. First of all, the Church tells us, we are to rejoice because "the Lord is most high, He is terrible (awe-inspiring); He is A GREAT KING OVER ALL THE EARTH" (Introit). And in the second place, this Great King has freed us from slavery to Satan, has chosen us as His children and destined us for eternal joy with Him and all His saints. To use our Lord's own imagery, as a divine gardener, He has planted us in His garden the Church where we have our "fruit unto sanctification, and our end, life everlasting" (Epistle).

Not only does God plant us in His garden (by

199

Baptism), He nurtures us and makes us strong, fruitful trees by bringing us into contact with the life-giving stream that flows through the center of the garden (the Eucharist). The source of that stream is the Sacrifice of Christ on Calvary, and its re-enacting and application to us takes place each time we offer up Holy Mass and receive Holy Communion. In this garden we are to grow and bring forth fruit.

Fruit trees either bear good fruit, evil fruit, or no fruit at all. So with us. We bear no fruit at all when we allow ourselves to become lukewarm mediocre Catholics ("I will vomit them out of my mouth," says our Lord). We bear evil fruit when we "yield our members to serve uncleanness and iniquity unto iniquity, the end of which is death" (Epistle).

Finally, we can bring forth good fruit. The good fruit which Christ wants us to bring forth — and which He does everything in His power to promote — is *holiness*, which at final harvest will mean for us life everlasting. This holiness is the rich colorful goodness of purity of life, courage, cheerful trust in God, patient kindliness towards our neighbor. It is union with God through union with Christ; it is total obedience to the recommendation of St. Paul that we heard so often during Holy Week: "Have this mind in you which was also in Christ Jesus."

THE WILL OF THE FATHER

And we are to bear this good fruit of holiness by doing the will of God. We must first of all want to do

God's will, and that is not easy. It is the old story that we have so often heard. For a tree to bear fruit, it has to expose itself to the sun, the rain, the wind, and to the prunings and cuttings of the gardener. So must we lay ourselves open to God's working in us. The sun of His love and its demands (especially when it requires love of neighbor) may seem too warm at times; the wind of His will may bend us almost to breaking; the prunings of pain, sickness, suffering of all kinds, separation from loved ones may seem well nigh unbearable. But these things are necessary for us. There is no good fruit without them.

"Not everyone who says to me, 'Lord, Lord,' shall enter the kingdom of heaven; but *he who does the will of my Father* in heaven shall enter the kingdom of heaven" (Gospel). Sweet words and pious thoughts that are not backed up by a real desire to do the will of the Father are so much breeze rustling through the leaves.

We express our willingness to do His will, to expose ourselves to His working in us, at Holy Hass. We manifest this willingness when we offer bread and wine, gifts symbolic of all that we have, are, and want to be. As we offer, we think in our hearts: "So let our sacrifice be made in Thy sight this day that it may please Thee" (Offertory verse). And when the bread and wine become the Body and Blood of Christ, we are drawn into the sacrificing, worshipping Christ. We become intimate sharers in His desire to do the will of His Father, sharers, too, in the sacrifice of Himself by which He outwardly expressed His desire to do His Father's will.

Only by sacrifice, by sacrifice made into an enduring frame of mind, can we do the will of the Father in heaven. Only by entering into Christ's sacrifice at Holy Mass can we bring forth fruits of holiness. Whether we are laymen, priests, or religious, as Christians we have but one vocation: to bring to maturity the divine Life we have received in Baptism, that is, to identify ourselves more and more with Christ, to become vitally living branches on Him, the true Vine.

The real test of holiness, of our fidelity to God's will, is our willingness to spend ourselves, our time, our love, our effort, in the apostolate. It takes more than one or two trees to make an orchard. God wills not only healthy trees, but more and more healthy trees. We are His instruments in bringing about that ideal. Our personal holiness will not only draw others (that is the way holiness acts), it will compel us to see our whole life in terms of Christ's world vision of salvation and sanctification.

Some day the Owner of the garden is going to make a tour of inspection. "By their fruits you will know them," He will say to Himself. We ought to be very much concerned about the results of that inspection. Will we stand the test of His appraising glance from the standpoint of our personal holiness as well as of the effort we have to put into the apostolate? Or will we have to shudder at His Verdict: "Every tree that does not bear good fruit is cut down and thrown into the fire"? We will not have to worry about fruit if we only come to realize that only God can make a tree and keep it fruitful.

FOOD FOR THE WAY

1. The wages of sin is death, but the gift of God is life everlasting in Christ Jesus our Lord (Epistle).

2. Not everyone who says to me, 'Lord, Lord,' shall enter the kingdom of heaven; but he who does the will of my Father in heaven shall enter the kingdom of heaven (Gospel).

3. There is no confusion to them that trust in Thee, O Lord (Offertory verse).

EIGHTH SUNDAY AFTER
PENTECOST

GIVE AN ACCOUNT

The unjust, dishonest steward of today's Gospel was apparently a very clever fellow. About to be dismissed by his master, he got himself into the good graces of the master's debtors so that he would be taken care of when out of work. He was looking out for number one. "And the master commended the unjust steward, in that he had acted prudently" (Gospel). Our Lord did not mean to praise dishonesty. But he did want to point out a very important lesson to us.

The lesson is this: just as the dishonest steward was wise in preparing for his later unemployment, so we should see to it that our life in the next world is taken care of just as surely; for some day each one of us will hear those same words: "Make an accounting of thy stewardship, for thou canst be steward no longer."

What is it that we are responsible for and which will one day require an accounting? It is our lives in this world as SONS OF GOD. We are God's sons. There can be no doubt about that after hearing today's Epistle: "You have received a spirit of adoption as sons, by virtue

204

of which we cry, 'Abba! Father!' The Spirit himself gives testimony to our spirit that we are sons of God. But if we are sons, we are heirs also: heirs indeed of God and joint heirs with Christ."

God is our Father, because we have received Life from Him. He lives in us. St. Paul calls us "adopted" sons of God, but God does more than give us His name and make us His heirs as is the case in human adoption. He gives us His LIFE. He makes us to share in His nature. This magnificent divine gift came to us in Baptism. "We have received Thy mercy, O God, in the midst of Thy temple" (Introit). We are laymen and women, religious, priests. But we are all sons of God! "Behold what manner of love the Father hath bestowed on us, that we should be called children of God: and such we are" (1 John 3:1). "But if we are sons, we are heirs also : heirs indeed of God and joint heirs with Christ" (Epistle).

LIVING AS GOD'S SONS

Our first reaction — it should develop into a life-long attitude — to God's mercy and love must be one of praiseful gratitude. "Great is the Lord, and exceedingly to be praised; in the city of our God, in His holy mountain" (Alleluia verse).

Then we must desire and resolve to do everything in our power to develop the divine Life we have received, to become more and more like unto Christ our Brother, the only-begotten Son of God, lest it be reported to our Father that we have unjustly "squandered

His possessions." That is what these Sundays after Pentecost are all about: growth in divine Life, preparing for the final harvest of the Last Judgment. We are sons of the most high God, of Him who is King and Lord of heaven and earth. Noble birth imposes the obligation of noble living.

But we have our difficulties. It is not easy to live up to our nobility, for we are still subject to sin, and we live in an atmosphere of worldliness that scorns God, His way of life, and spiritual gifts He promises. Christ's timely warning that we shall have to give an accounting, and St. Paul's frightening words in the Epistle cause no more than a momentary hesitation to our world... and even to us who should know better: "If you live according to the flesh you will die: but if by the spirit you put to death the deeds of the flesh, you will live" (Epistle).

Threats are necessary, they are good for us, and the Church sees to it in these Sunday Masses that we are reminded frequently enough of the end that awaits those who fail to live up to their vocation as children of God. But threats are negative. Fear of God's wrath alone will not bring about holy living. "Whoever are led by the Spirit of God, they are the sons of God. Now you have not received a spirit of *bondage so as to be again in fear*, but you have received a spirit of adoption as sons." Fear must be implemented by love. God is a Father, the best, the most perfect, of Fathers. A father does not want to be feared by his children, he wants to be loved. Which is why we pray so earnestly today: "O Lord, in Thy mercy grant us the spirit of always thinking and doing what is right, so that we who cannot exist without Thee, may be able *to live according to Thy will*" (Collect).

There has to be contact, mutual trust and confidence, between father and sons; otherwise they drift apart and live their own lives. There must also be contact between us and God our Father. We have to speak to Him, confide in Him, trust in Him, to "taste and see that the Lord is sweet: blessed is the man that hopeth in Him" (Communion verse). We can maintain this contact by *prayer*, especially by a prayerful frame of mind (the basis of which is self-dedication to His will).

Thus, one of the best prayers at our command is similar to a child's admiring looking-into-the-eyes of his father — it is gift of self to our God, trusting abandon of all that we are and hope to be and do unto our Father's care. This was Christ's way of keeping in touch with His Father all His life. We should try to make it our way, too.

Living according to our Father's will means, therefore, total gift of self to Him. It is this gift that wins greater graces of sonship for ourselves and for those whom He wants us to attract to Him by our apostolate. "The will of the Father is that every creature turn to His glory, that every human voice sing His praises by coming to know Christ and to be united to Him. How can we be united to this holy will and not espouse His desire? How can we espouse His desire and not act with all our strength in spreading the love of Christ for the glory of His Father" (Père Lochet)? God grant that we will all be able to make a good accounting of the stewardship of our life as God's sons *and* our life as His apostles!

FOOD FOR THE WAY

1. In Thee, O God, have I hoped: let me never be confounded (Alleluia verse).
2. Who is God but Thee, O Lord (Offertory verse)?
3. Taste and see that the Lord is sweet: blessed is the man that Hopeth in Him (Communion verse).

NINTH SUNDAY AFTER PENTECOST

THE TIME OF VISITATION

The fear theme that we noticed last Sunday is strongly accented today in both Epistle and Gospel. We insist that the Church is more concerned about urging and helping us to live positive lives of loving service of God than with holding over our heads frightening threats that would keep us doing the minimum to avoid damnation. However, the Church would fail in her all-round maternal vigilance if she did not remind us occasionally of the truth that we are not yet saved, and that the mere fact of our Baptism and membership in Christ does not yet guarantee our salvation.

Her method today is to set forth the object lesson of the Chosen Race of the Old Testament, saying to us: "Brethren, these things came to pass as examples to us, that we should not lust after evil things" (Epistle). Worshipping the false gods of body and sense pleasures, thinking and acting as though God did not exist, impurity of all sorts, tempting God by seeing how far they could go in sinning — all these crimes brought punishing death on many of the Chosen People.

209

They had the God-given mission to prepare themselves for the coming of the Savior so that they could give Him to the world. But He came into His own and His own received Him not. Towards the end of His life of struggle with their leaders to make them see that Redemption was a spiritual rather than a political blessing, "Jesus drew near to Jerusalem and saw the city and wept over it saying 'If thou hadst known, in this thy day, even thou, the things that are for thy peace! But now they are hidden from thy eyes. For days will come upon thee when thy enemies will throw up a rampart about thee, and surround thee and shut thee in on every side, and will dash thee to the ground and thy children within thee, and will not leave in thee one stone upon another, because thou hast not known the time of thy visitation.' And He entered the temple, and began to cast out those who are selling and buying in it, saying to them, 'It is written, My house is a house of prayer, but you have made it a den of thieves' " (Gospel).

CHRIST WEEPING OVER US

"Now all these things happened to them as a type, and they were written for our correction, upon whom the final age of the world has come" (Epistle). We are now the chosen people. We now have the mission to receive the Savior, to grow in union with Him, so that we can bring Him forth to our world. Today Mother Church wants us to re-examine our fidelity to our vocation as a people and as individual members of the Christian Community.

We have God as our God and our Father: "Behold, God is my helper, and the Lord is the protector of my soul" (Introit). We have Christ as our Savior, our Mediator with the Father, "teaching us daily in the temple" through the Gospel. We have in Holy Mass the very sacrifice that He offered for us on Calvary. "Every time this memorial Sacrifice is offered up, the work of our redemption is carried on" (Secret). We have Holy Communion, the fruit of the Sacrifice, in which He feeds us with His own Body and Blood. "He who eats My flesh, and drinks My blood, abides in me, and I in him" (Communion verse).

We can say as the Old Testament people never could with so much truth: "O Lord, our Lord, how wonderful is Thy Name in the whole earth" (Gradual). "The justices of the Lord are right, rejoicing hearts, and His judgments are sweeter than honey and the honeycomb" (Offertory verse).

But if we do not keep these judgments, if God is only a far-off Name to us, if we say these prayers with our lips, with our hearts far from Him; if Christ is only an historical figure whom we do not allow into our present day thinking and living; if we do not participate in His Sacrifice actively and intelligently both singly and as a people; if we do not permit Communion to purify our hearts and unite us more intimately one with another (Postcommunion prayer); if we are provincial and narrow and selfishly individualistic about our faith instead of doing everything in our power to manifest that faith to the world as a saving faith; if we practice race prejudice and segregation in our relation with others — if we do all these things, then we can be sure that Christ is weeping over us just as surely as He wept over Jerusalem... and for the same reason: we have not known the time of *our* visitation.

HOUSE OF PRAYER

Again we say, our lives are not to be motivated by fear but by love and trust. We are God's people, unworthy though we be, and He is our Helper and Protector. But, says the Church *"let him who thinks he stands take heed* lest he fall. May no temptation take hold of you but such as man is equal to. God is faithful and will not permit you to be tempted beyond your strength" (Epistle).

"My house is a house of prayer." We are Christ's houses. We belong to Him. He dwells in us, making us houses of prayer. These houses of prayer must not become dens of thieves, filled with all manner of evil, complaining, and uncharitable thoughts, calling forth the tears of Christ. No, they must rather be houses of salvation for us and for others who become our guests through our apostolic contacts. "How lovely are Thy tabernacles, O Lord of Hosts! my soul longeth and fainteth for the courts of the Lord. My heart and my flesh have rejoiced in the living God... Blessed are they that dwell in Thy house, O Lord: they shall praise Thee for ever and ever" (Psalm 83:2, 3, 5). "The temple of God is holy, and this temple you are" (1 Corinthians 3:17). This is the proper prayer for us who are temples of God and houses of prayer: "Let Thy merciful ears, O Lord, be open to the prayers of Thy lowly petitioners,

212

and in order to satisfy their desires, make them *ask such things as are pleasing to Thee"* (Collect). The things most pleasing to our God are the souls of men.

FOOD FOR THE WAY

1. Save me, O God, by Thy Name, and deliver me in Thy strength (Introit).

2. O Lord, our Lord, how admirable is Thy Name in the whole earth (Gradual)!

3. The justices of the Lord are right, rejoicing hearts, and His judgments sweeter than honey and the honeycomb: for Thy servant keepeth them (Offertory verse).

TENTH SUNDAY AFTER PENTECOST

BUT THE SAME SPIRIT

In a parish there are housewives, doctors, laborers, teachers, farmers, business men, musicians, priests, sisters, taxi and bus-drivers, undertakers, students, and all manner of professional men and women. Let no one be slighted at not finding his profession listed; for no profession is unimportant. In the words of today's Epistle: "There are varieties of gifts but the same Spirit; and there are varieties of ministries, but the same Lord; and there are varieties of workings, but *the same God, who works all things in all.*"

Each one of us has his particular vocation — given by God Himself, in fidelity to which we find salvation and sanctification for ourselves. And if all members are faithful to all the variety of vocations, the parish community which they compose will find salvation and sanctification and, most important of all, will attract those outside to its way of life.

Christ, St. Paul, and holy Church insist repeatedly of the all-importance of the community. Their insistence needs to be emphasized in these days of individualism.

Our parishes, and the whole Church, will become good working units only when each member puts heart and will into the excellent performance of the work demanded by each vocation. On the other hand, when the members lose sight of the good of the whole, and their individual obligations to the good of the whole, the unit will tend to split up. Instead of a single organism working together for a common purpose, there is an indefinite number of prima donnas all working for their own singular glory, saying in their hearts, "O God, I thank thee that I am not like the rest of men" (Gospel).

THE OIL OF HUMILITY

Today's Mass is concerned with the smooth, efficient functioning of Christ's Community, the Church. In the Gospel our Lord pictures two men for our meditation. The one can destroy the community, the other can save and build it up. The Pharisee, pride and selfishness incarnate, who sets himself apart from the community and above it, is a ridiculous figure, but also pitiful and terrifying. Pride is a wretched fault when we see what it does to a person, but it is much more vicious when we see what it does to a community.

What is disturbing is that there is a bit of the Pharisee in all of us. No one is immune to the virus; and one of our life-long tasks is to replace his haughty, self-seeking attitude with the humble, self-forgetful philosophy of the publican: "O God, be merciful to me the sinner!" The publican was humble, and humility works for the well-being of the entire community in the same way that oil provides smooth running in a machine.

215

A person is said to be humble when he knows the truth about himself, about his position in the community, and about God. First of all, the truth about himself: he knows that he is not self-sufficient. He knows that all that he is, all the good he does, is God's working within him. "Without me, you can do nothing," our Lord said, and the humble man believes it. The only thing he can call his own are his sins, his neglect of God's grace.

Second, the humble man knows the truth about his position in the community. He realizes that he is like an organ in a body. It may be a very insignificant organ, but it is necessary to the health and even functioning of the body. He depends on the whole body for his life and health and in turn contributes his share to the well-being of the whole. Without the community and its life-giving Spirit, he becomes an outcast, in danger of perishing. He does his work well, no matter how humble it may seem to him or to others, because God so wills it. "But all these things are the work of one and the same Spirit, who divides to everyone according as he will" (Epistle).

Third, the humble man knows the truth about God. In spite of all his failings, he knows that God remains his Father, that his Father loves him, that when he cries to the Lord, the Lord will hear his voice and will not despise his humble supplication (Introit). Realizing his helplessness without God, he casts all his care upon the Lord who sustains him. "To Thee, O Lord, have I lifted up my soul: in Thee, O my God, I put my trust, let me not be ashamed: neither let my enemies laugh at me: for none of them that wait on Thee shall be confounded" (Offertory verse).

216

THE APPLE OF GOD'S EYE

It does not matter how insignificant our position in the community may seem to us. What does matter is that we are in the Community of Christ and that we do our best to bring others into it also. God loves us for what we are. He loves the humble man because the humble man loves God more than himself, loves the community more than self-glory. The proud man closes his heart to the working of God's grace. The Holy Spirit of loving unity circulating through the body runs up against the proud man and is stopped. But the humble man is a good conductor of the Spirit: he is ever open to His fullness.

O GOD, BE MERCIFUL TO ME A SINNER! This prayer of the humble publican should be in our hearts always. It is not a prayer of tragic despair, but of firm confidence. "When I cried to the Lord He heard my voice... Hear, O God, my prayer, and despise not my supplication; be attentive to me and hear me" (Introit). Thus does the humble man pray. Knowing himself, knowing his position in the community, knowing God, the humble man becomes as a little child. And of such is the kingdom of heaven.

FOOD FOR THE WAY

1. Keep me, O Lord, as the apple of Thy eye: protect me under the shadow of Thy wings (Gradual).
2. O God, be merciful to me the sinner (Gospel).
3. Everyone who exalts himself shall be humbled, and he who humbles himself shall be exalted (Gospel).

ELEVENTH SUNDAY AFTER PENTECOST

WORKING AT OUR BAPTISM

In these post-Pentecost Masses there is nearly always some reference to Easter and to one or the other aspect of Easter's baptismal renewal. Some might wonder why there is so much insistence on Baptism, and whether, instead of reminding us continually of that far-off event, it would not be better for the Church to give us something more practical for our modern life and all its problems.

The fact is that everything that happens to us in a spiritual way dates back directly to our Baptism and to its renewal in us this year at Easter. As was mentioned before in these pages, Baptism is more than a stationary event in the personal history of each of us. It is a conversion from evil to God that must become a way of life for us all.

Today's Gospel, for example, treats of the power Baptism gives us *to speak* to God and *to hear* His answer. "They brought to him one deaf and dumb, and entreated him to lay his hand upon him. And taking him aside from the crowd, he put his fingers into the man's ears, and spitting, he touched his tongue. And he said to him, 'Ephpheta,' that is, 'Be thou opened.' And his ears were at once opened, and the bond of his tongue was loosed, and he began to speak correctly" (Gospel). This man is the image of us all.

Before Baptism we were deaf and dumb as far as contacts with God were concerned. We could neither hear Him nor speak to Him aright. Not to be able to speak to our Father and to hear His voice in blessed answer is much worse than not to be able to hear or speak to men. Today, and in other Post-Pentecost Masses, Mother Church reminds us of our abilities in these respects and urges us to *practice* these abilities. She is the one who really is practical.

MY FLESH FLOURISHED AGAIN

Back in World War II there was a good deal of talk and sermonizing about the scarcity of atheists in foxholes and planes. Prayer became a rather popular pastime when death threatened momentarily; for then men realized that "self-confidence alone was not enough to sustain the human spirit" *(Reader's Digest*, July 1942).

"In God hath my heart confided, *and I have been helped:* and my flesh hath flourished again; and with my will I will give praise to Him. Unto Thee will I cry, O Lord: O my God, be not then silent; depart not from me" (Gradual). Probably few if any combat men used those words, but could any have been more appropriate? In their trouble they confided in the Lord, they were helped, and their "flesh flourished again."

The power of speaking to God and hearing Him is one of His most precious gifts to us. But the power has to be used, not only when we are in difficulty, but every day. It is only by daily practice in speaking to and confiding in God that we can prepare ourselves to hear His comforting words in our own life battles.

We know and have been told often enough that we can practice this power simply by talking to God in our own words at any time, talking to Him as we would to a good friend, telling Him our needs, thanking Him for His favors and past helps, and above all, telling Him how much we love Him and how much He means to us. "In God hath my *heart* confided." It is our Baptism that gives us the right to say: "I will extol Thee, O Lord, for thou has upheld me; and hast not made my enemies to rejoice over me: O Lord, I have cried to Thee, and Thou hast healed me" (Offertory verse).

Our best chance to practice our power is at Holy Mass. We can speak to God when we pray the Introit, Collect, Kyrie, Gloria, Gradual, and Offertory verse. In these prayers we are made aware of our helplessness and beg for mercy; we praise and glorify Him; we plead with Him for help to be true to Him. He in turn speaks to us in the Epistle and Gospel, "by which we are being saved, *if we hold it fast,*" as St. Paul reminds us in to-day's Epistle.

BE THOU OPENED

But God does more than speak to us at Mass. He who died, who rose again from the dead, who appeared

220

to the apostles (see the Epistle), appears to us. And together with us, He offers up the same saving sacrifice that He offered on Calvary.

At Holy Mass it is with Christ in our midst that we confide in God, that we rejoice in God our helper and sing aloud to Him (Alleluia verse). He is in our very midst when He gives Himself to us in Holy Communion. We know what He wants to do in us. He wants to do what He did to the deaf-mute, what He did to us at our Baptism. "Be *thou* opened," He says to *us*.

Sin may have stopped our ears to God's voice. Our neglect of prayer may have made us dumb and incapable of speaking our needs and singing His praises. We may very well be in a prison of spiritual deafness and dumbness, inclosed in walls of thick despair. But here we are at Mass, and it is never too late. Christ can break through the thickest walls with a little help from within. He says to us today: "Be thou opened, and stay opened. Practice your powers. Speak to your Father daily, vocally and mentally, *confide in Him*, and your flesh shall flourish again."

What St. Paul said, we can say: "By the grace of God I am what I am" (Epistle). Christ has chosen us, has touched our ears and tongues. He has done all things well. But can we claim as St. Paul could: "His grace in me has not been fruitless"? That depends on our zeal in the apostolate, which in turn depends on our prayer life and union with God. It is all quite simple: "Honor the Lord with thy substance (i.e., your love, your trust, your efforts, your whole being): and thy barns shall be filled with abundance and thy presses shall run over with wine" (Communion verse). It is God who gives the increase.

1. Rejoice to God our helper; sing aloud to the God of Jacob: take a pleasant psalm with the harp (Alleluia verse).

2. He has done all things well. He has made both the deaf to hear and the dumb to speak (Gospel).

3. O Lord, I have cried to Thee, and Thou hast healed me (Offertory verse).

TWELFTH SUNDAY AFTER PENTECOST

THE BIG QUESTION

"Master, what must I do to gain eternal life?" The years that have passed since that question was first asked have not changed the importance either of the question or its answer. "Thou shalt love the Lord thy God with thy whole heart, and with thy whole soul, and with thy whole strength, and with thy whole mind; and thy neighbor as thyself" (Gospel).

We are to do just that: love God with a total love. And love our neighbor as ourself. Then and only then will we know what life and happiness and peace really are. We are to love God because He has first loved us, because He has saved us and has kept us saved. But He Himself tells us the dramatic story of His love for us in today's Gospel parable.

The man who went from Jerusalem to Jericho and fell among robbers (who stripped him and left him half dead) is the human race in general and each of us in particular. The Old Testament, in the persons of the priest and Levite, passed us by, unable to save us. Then came the Good Samaritan, Jesus Christ. Moved with

223

compassion for us, He bound up our wounds, pouring oil and wine upon them, and brought us to the Inn. "Take care of him," He said to the innkeeper, "And I on my way back, will repay thee."

INN-MATES THAT WE ARE

TAKE CARE OF HIM. These are key words for understanding Christ's far-reaching work of love for us. He was not satisfied with pouring into our wounded, God-starved souls the oil and wine of His grace, won for us by His death on Calvary. His work of saving mankind goes on and on. The victim's wounds have to be healed; he must convalesce, must build up resistance against further attacks of the great robber, Satan.

Christ saw to all that by making reservations for us in the Inn which is His Church. He established a place of refuge for us and paid the price: He died for us. We are in Christ's Inn today. "Such assurance I have through Christ towards God. Not that we are sufficient of ourselves to think anything as from ourselves, but our sufficiency is from God" (Epistle).

As long as we stay in this Inn, we are safe. But we must fall in with the Inn's way of life, its order of the day. Included in this way of life is mealtime and our relations to our fellow inn-mates. Mealtime, we know, is holy Mass, the Sacrifice of Calvary and the Last Supper renewed for us. Here Christ continues to pour into our wounds the oil and wine of divine Grace. Here are His words fulfilled in us: "Blessed are the eyes that see what you see" (Gospel).

But the lasting benefits we receive from this Oil and Wine of divine Grace depend greatly on the attitude we cultivate towards the heavenly Innkeeper, Almighty God, and towards our fellow guests in His Inn. Towards God it is ever an attitude of love, gratitude, and praise. "Thou shalt love the Lord thy God *with thy whole heart, with all thy strength.*" This total love of God is a supernatural gift, it comes from God, and we have to pray for it constantly. "O Almighty and Eternal God, by Whose gift Thy faithful are able to serve Thee worthily and praiseworthily, grant, we pray Thee, that we may run without stumbling to the fulfillment of Thy promises" (Collect). "I will bless the Lord at all times; His praise shall be ever in my mouth. In the Lord shall my soul be praised: let the meek hear, and rejoice" (Gradual).

Total love for God is total gift of self to Him; it is spending ourselves and our substance in praise of God and in gratitude to Him, just as our Good Samaritan did for us. This is the whole law. When with Christ we can say about our God, "I do always the things that please Him" (John 8:29), then we truly love Him. Love is a bond that binds us to God and keeps us bound for all eternity. But this love has to have its beginning in this world.

It has to have its beginning in our relations to our neighbor. St. John writes so accurately: "Let us therefore love, because God first loved us. If anyone says, 'I love God' and hates his brother, he is a liar. For how can he who does not love his brother, whom he sees, love God, whom he does not see? And this commandment we have from him, that he who loves God should love his brother also" (1 John 4:20-21).

But who is our neighbor? It is he who has fallen among robbers and has not yet been rescued. Our neighbor is anyone who is poor, anyone who is pagan, anyone who is sick, homeless, wounded, suffering, anyone who does not know he is loved. In short, our neighbor is everyone; but above all, the person right next to us. Because Christ was a Good Samaritan to us, we must be good samaritans to our fellow men, doing for them exactly what Christ did for us. The recognition of our neighbor as precious in the eyes of Christ is one of the great needs of our age.

The love of Christ has never ceased. It has continued in His Church. So also is His love for others continued in us. This is a wonderful thing: that when we love others and help them in any way, it is not our own love exclusively, *it is Christ's love finding its present-day channel into our world through us.* He is our Good Samaritan; He wants us to be His stand-ins in our world. We are in His Inn, present today at His Sacrifice. "I will bless the Lord at all times, His praise shall ever be in my mouth" (Gradual). But there are so many of our fellow men who are not with us!

MASTER, WHAT MUST I DO TO GAIN ETERNAL LIFE? We must love. When we learn that, then "The earth shall be filled with the fruit of Thy works, O Lord, that Thou mayest bring bread out of the earth, and that wine may cheer the heart of man;

that he may make the face cheerful with oil; and that bread may strengthen man's heart" (Communion verse).

FOOD FOR THE WAY

1. Incline unto my aid, O God: O Lord, make haste to help me (Introit).

2. Blessed are the eyes that see the things that you see (Gospel)!

3. Thou shalt love the Lord thy God with thy whole heart... and with thy whole mind; and thy neighbor as thyself (Gospel).

THIRTEENTH SUNDAY AFTER PENTECOST

THEY WERE MADE CLEAN

In a dozen different ways the Church, in these Sunday Masses, has been dramatizing for us our condition as baptized followers and members of Christ and thus trying to drive home to us the way of life that should flow out of the new nature we have by His grace.

Thus, we are the lost sheep whom the Good Shepherd rescued and brought back into His sheepfold (Third Sunday after Pentecost); we are passengers in Peter's ship (Fourth Sunday); we are trees planted in Christ's garden which He cultivates so that they will bring forth fruit (Seventh Sunday); we were rescued from the great robber Satan by the Good Samaritan, Christ, and brought into His Inn the Church, where all our needs are taken care of (Twelfth Sunday).

Most dramatic of all is today's Gospel description of the change that our Lord worked in us by Baptism and the personal, life-long response that we ought to have to His great love for us. "There met him ten lepers, who stood afar off and lifted up their voice, crying, 'Jesus, master, have pity on us.' And when he saw

228

them he said, 'Go, show yourselves to the priests.' And it came to pass that, as they were on their way, they were made clean."

Men who at one moment were carriers of the deadliest, most horrible of diseases, living death, were the next moment changed, filled with new life, made clean and healthy. And all because Christ looked upon them, took pity on them, loved them and heard their piteous plea.

Before our Baptism we were carriers of worse than living death. Leprosy of the body gives only a faint idea of what sin is in the soul, be it original sin or sin committed personally now. But Christ took pity on us and healed us. "Go, show yourselves to the priests." Living death of sin gave way to an onrush of fresh, new Life. God Himself became our Life, our Health. And not only did He cleanse us. He brought us into His Home, the Church, where, in order to keep us from relapse and to help us to grow in health, He "gave us bread from heaven, having in it all that is delicious and the sweetness of every taste" (Communion verse).

WITH A LOUD VOICE

However, all that is only half the story. "But one of them seeing that he was made clean, returned, with a loud voice glorifying God, and he fell on his face at his feet, giving thanks" (Gospel).

Only one out of ten had enough character to return and thank our Lord. But he did it so well that we need never look for a better example of the reaction that we should have to God's mercy to us. Notice what the man did: *with a loud voice* he glorified God, fell on his knees, giving thanks. That is exactly what we must do at every Mass. But we must do it with a loud voice and falling on our knees, in other words, by *active* participation of all our human faculties of mind, heart, and body.

The Christian life, therefore, must be a thankful life. We know that from Christ's attitude: "Were not ten made clean? Where are the nine?" Gratitude is essential to our continued growth in health (holiness). But there is no better expression of gratitude than Holy Mass and Communion. The word "Eucharist" comes from a Greek word meaning "thanksgiving." At Mass our thanksgiving is Christ Himself.

We may fall back into leprosy, into sin. In fact, the Church seems almost to expect it: her Mass is full of prayers that fit only in the mouths of sinners. "Have regard, O Lord, to Thy covenant, and forsake not to the end the souls of Thy poor: arise, O Lord, and judge Thy cause, and forget not the voices of them that seek Thee" (Introit). Kyrie eleison... Lord have mercy, Christ have mercy, Lord have mercy. But if our lives are Eucharistic, that is, grateful and sacrificial, our purification will steadily progress unto final unchangeable union with Him.

"In Thee, O Lord, have I hoped: I said, Thou art my God, my times are in Thy hands," so do we pray as we get ready to express our gratitude by offering our whole beings to Him at the offering of bread and wine. My times — my days in the apostolate, my hours in the field, at the office, in the home, at school, all my work, my whole being — all this is in Thy hands.

"Look with favor upon Thy people, O Lord; look with favor upon their gifts and, being appeased by this offering, mercifully grant us pardon for our sins and the blessings that we ask" (Secret). God will not fail to answer an appeal that so sincerely acknowledges Him as "our refuge from generation unto generation" (Alleluia verse). "Let us give thanks to the Lord," the priest urges us at the Preface. And we answer with full hearts: "It is truly meet and just."

Now in the Sacrifice God turns to us. He will not take away our pain and grief, for we are Christians, followers of Him who carried His cross and made the cross a part of all our lives. But He will and does take away the despairing wretchedness of those who do not know Christ and who therefore can hardly know any relief from their pain. He will give us "Bread from Heaven, having in it all that is delicious, and the sweetness of every taste" (Communion verse); and when we have eaten that Bread, we will experience an increase of our hope of eternal salvation.

In the Collect we pray: "Grant us an increase of faith, hope, and charity; and that we may deserve what Thou dost promise, make us love what Thou dost command." But what does He command? "Do this in commemoration of me." He commands the Eucharist. To fulfill that command, to fulfill it as the Samaritan did, "with a loud voice, falling on his knees glorifying God, giving thanks," will be to hear Christ's consoling voice: "Arise, go thy way." Ite, Missa est. The Mass is ended.

231

But we go into another week purified, strengthened, filled with new life. "Thy faith has saved thee" (Gospel).

FOOD FOR THE WAY

1. Lord, Thou hast been our refuge, from generation to generation (Alleluia verse).

2. In Thee, O Lord, have I hoped: I said, Thou art my God, my times are in Thy hands.

3. Thou hast given us, O Lord, bread from heaven, having in it all that is delicious, and the sweetness of every taste. (Communion verse).

FOURTEENTH SUNDAY AFTER PENTECOST

SPIRIT AND FLESH

There is more in today's Mass about the deep nature of man — his needs and urges and the means of satisfying those needs — than in libraries of books on psychiatry. We are told that man is body and soul, flesh and spirit, and that these two are in conflict one with the other. "The flesh lusts against the spirit, and the spirit against the flesh; for these are opposed to each other, so that you do not do what you would" (Epistle).

We have all experienced that struggle and know the consequences of giving in to the one side or the other: "Now the works of the flesh are manifest, which are immorality, uncleanness, licentiousness, idolatry, witchcrafts, enmities, jealousies, anger, quarrels, murders, drunkenness, carousings, and suchlike. And concerning these I warn you... that they who do such things will not attain the kingdom of God" (Epistle).

St. Paul scarcely needs to indicate the final outcome of a life of giving in to the demands of the flesh: the desperate sense of futility and boredom. Man is body-spirit. Spirit also has its needs; and the more man tries to satisfy his spirit with material things, the greater will be the awful feeling of emptiness within him.

Father Leen says it this way: "Nothing can fill up the infinite capacity in the human soul except what can physically enter into it and take possession of it, and this privilege belongs to the Creator alone, and to that participation in His life which is given in grace and glory. 'Thou hast made us for Thee, O Lord, and our hearts are restless till they rest in Thee.' Nothing but God and the life of God can enter the human soul, and therefore nothing but God can still the restlessness" (*Progress Through Mental Prayer*, p. 126).

GOD AND MAMMON

In the Gospel our Lord makes this truth very clear: "You cannot serve God and mammon." We cannot live a worldly life and a spiritual life at the same time. The body does have its needs. Men with families do have to work hard to provide for all that is necessary to their life. Laziness is sinful. There are natural problems which have to be met. But what Christ does condemn is undue worry that causes lack of trust in the loving providing of our Father, "Who knows that you need all these things. But seek first the kingdom of God and His justice, and all these things shall be given you besides."

In other words, "It is good to confide in the Lord, rather than to have confidence in man. It is good to trust in the Lord, rather than to trust in princes. Alleluia, alleluia. Come, let us praise the Lord with joy; let us joyfully sing to God our Savior" (Gradual and Alleluia). Confiding in God and praising Him — that is seeking His kingdom, that is living according to the spirit, that is Christianity. And that is essential also in the apostolate.

The fruit of the Spirit is: charity, joy, peace, patience, kindness, goodness, longsuffering, mildness, faith, modesty, continency, chastity. Against such things there is no law" (Epistle).

It is a difficult decision to make — to live according to the flesh or the spirit — and once we have made it, even more difficult to carry out. Trust in God is easy to preach about to others, but hard to practice oneself, especially when the demands of the body press hard for satisfaction or when a frightening crisis threatens oneself or one's family.

HOW LOVELY ARE THY TABERNACLES

Our attempts to live up to the ideal of the primacy of the spiritual may fall far short of success simply because it is a life-long work. What is tragic is not to know the ideal. SEEK FIRST THE KINGDOM OF GOD. "Here is the uncompromising surrender demanded of our faith; and only the supernatural man, the man who thinks as a Christian, can understand it" (Loehr: *The Year of Our Lord*, p. 299).

The best way, in fact, one of the only ways, to become a supernatural man, a man who thinks as a true Christian, is to pray these Sunday Masses to the hilt, to allow oneself to become impregnated by their spirit.

235

Man cannot sin, he will not be over anxious about material security, if he is filled with God. "Behold, O God, our Protector, and look on the face of Thy anointed one: for better is one day in Thy courts above thousands. How lovely are Thy tabernacles, O Lord of Hosts! My soul longeth and fainteth for the courts of the Lord" (Introit).

Praying these Sunday Masses makes us talk that way, makes us recognize our helplessness without Him, our great longing for Him, and requires us to pray: "Guard Thy Church, we implore Thee, O Lord, with thy perpetual mercy and, since without Thee our human weakness is every ready to fall, by Thy help always keep it from all things harmful and lead it to all things helpful to our salvation" (Collect).

Praying these Sunday Masses year after year works the conversion in us which gives us the strength "to crucify our flesh with its passions and desires" (Epistle); it "purifies and strengthens us at all times and leads us to the fruit of everlasting salvation" (Postcommunion). But best of all, praying these Masses opens the way for God into our soul to the end that He possesses us and we possess Him. Then we can say: "O taste and see that the Lord is sweet (Offertory verse).

And when we have tasted and seen that the Lord is sweet, we will want to do all in our power to share our relish for Him with others. We shall have no worry about results in the apostolate or in our own spiritual life; for we shall have sought first the kingdom of God, and all these things shall be given to us besides.

FOOD FOR THE WAY

1. They who belong to Christ have crucified their flesh with its passions and desires (Epistle).

2. Look at the birds of the air... your heavenly Father feeds them. Are not you of much more value than they (Gospel)?

3. Come, let us praise the Lord with joy; let us joyfully sing to God our Savior (Alleluia verse).

FIFTEENTH SUNDAY AFTER PENTECOST

I. YOUNG MAN, I SAY TO THEE, ARISE

The young man they were carrying to the cemetery was her only son. She had poured out her life for him, and now he was taken from her. She would be alone. But suddenly the procession stops. Through her tears she sees a Man who says to her: "Do not weep." She hears Him speak to her dead son: "Young man, I say to thee, arise." And he who was dead sat up and began to speak. And the Man gave the son back to his mother (Gospel).

Then there came a great fear upon all the people in the procession, but not upon her. She was too full of joy and gratitude. "And they began to glorify God, saying, 'A great prophet has risen among us,' and 'God has visited his people.'"

II. YOUNG MAN, I SAY TO THEE, ARISE

Each of us as a child has been carried out in a similar procession. We probably gave loud evidence of natural life, but we were dead spiritually. The procession stopped at the baptismal font of our parish church. The Man of the above scene touched us and said to us: "Young man, I say to thee, arise."

And we who were dead sat up. We were re-born. We were able to say: "It is now no longer I that live, but *Christ lives in me*" (Galatians 2:20). It is the property of the spiritually alive to speak and sing God's praises.

And He delivered us to our new Mother, the Church, who glorified God saying: The great Prophet is still with us, and God continues to visit His people. "It is good to give praise to the Lord; and to sing to Thy Name, O Most High. To show forth Thy mercy in the morning, and Thy truth in the night. Alleluia. Alleluia. For the Lord is a great God, and a great King above all the earth" (Gradual and Alleluia verses).

III. YOUNG MAN, I SAY TO THEE, ARISE

It is the Fifteenth Sunday after Pentecost of this year of grace. "Bow down Thy ear, O Lord, to me, and hear me: save Thy servant, O my God, that trusteth in Thee: have mercy on me, O Lord, for I have cried to Thee all day." (Introit).

This is the prayer of a woman in mourning. It is the prayer of our Mother the Church. She is mourning the loss of her children, who, through mortal sin have fallen back into spiritual death — those who have not been true to their baptismal resurrection, who have sown in the flesh, from which they reap corruption (Epistle). She mourns also all those children who are still dead to her, those who have not yet been brought to her: the heathen, the heretics, all the unbaptized.

But hers is not a blind mourning like the grief of one who has no God. She knows that her great Prophet is still with her and that her prayer will be heard. She trusts in Him, knowing that He will "give joy to the soul of His servant; for to Thee, O Lord, have I lifted up my soul" (Introit).

Such a poignant and confident prayer will not go unheard. The Lord sees the grief of the Mother, and touched with compassion, He says: "Do not weep." And turning to us, her sons present around the altar, He says: "Young man, I say to you, arise."

ARISE AND LIVE

If you live by the Spirit, He says to us, by the Spirit you must also walk. Do not become desirous of vain glory, provoking one another, envying one another. You are a community, a family. You all have your work to do, your particular gifts from My Father. Bear one another's burdens and so you will fulfill My law. For if anyone thinks himself to be something, whereas he is nothing, he deceives himself. And in doing good, do not grow tired; for in due time you shall reap if you do not relax. The apostolate must go on. It will bear fruit, for it is My apostolate. Therefore, while you still have time, do good to all men, but especially to those who are of the household of the faith (Epistle).

It is Christ, through St. Paul, who thus urges us to

a complete Christian life. But if His positive urging (and above all, His own and our Mother Church's example) do not move us to determine upon a life of better cooperation with Him, perhaps this alarming threat will stir us up: "Be not deceived, God is not mocked. For what a man sows, that he will also reap. For he who sows in the flesh, from the flesh also he will reap corruption" (Epistle).

Young men, arise. Arise and live on this word of Christ, live according to the Spirit, according to the new life of praise and conquest He began in you at Baptism. Say with all your heart: "With expectation I have waited for the Lord, and He had regard to me; and He heard my prayer, and He put a new canticle in my mouth, a song to our God" (Offertory verse).

After we say that, we enter into His sacrifice, we go up unto His Life-giving, Life-increasing Cross with Him, we die with Him to our lower self. Then at Communion, made strong on the Bread of eternal Life that He gives to us, His flesh for the life of the world (Communion verse), we go forth into another week "defended against all the attacks of the evil one" (Secret).

FOOD FOR THE WAY

1. It is good to give praise to the Lord; and to sing to Thy Name, O Most High. To show forth Thy mercy in the morning, and Thy truth in the night (Gradual).
2. A great prophet has risen among us, and God has visited His people (Offertory verse).
3. The Bread that I will give is My flesh for the life of the world (Communion verse).

241

SIXTEENTH SUNDAY AFTER PENTECOST

UNTO PROGRESS OF THE INNER MAN

St. Paul converted and baptized thousands of pagans. But he was never satisfied, either with the numerical results or with the degree of union with God in his followers. To make his new Christians see their Baptism as a wholehearted dedication of themselves to God, a dedication based on vivid, generous love for Him — that he felt he could not do only by preaching. Something — and Someone — else was needed.

And so he prayed: "I bend my knees to the Father of our Lord Jesus Christ... that he may grant you from his glorious riches to be strengthened with power through his Spirit unto the progress of the inner man; and to have Christ dwelling by faith in your hearts: so that, being rooted and grounded in love, you may be able to comprehend with all the saints what is the breadth and length and height and depth, and to know Christ's love which surpasses all knowledge, in order that YOU MAY BE FILLED UNTO ALL THE FULLNESS OF GOD" (Epistle).

242

Holy Church has made St. Paul's prayer her own. It is now backed up by all the power of Christ her Head, therefore it shall be heard. The Church today prays for us, her children, that we may be filled unto all the fullness of God. That is the ideal of our Christian life: unto that Christ has called us all. The harvest time is approaching: the end of this year of grace, the end of this life of grace, the day when "the Lord shall be seen in his majesty" (Gradual).

NEEDY AND POOR

The vision of that final reckoning (it is a vision that will now become progressively more distinct until it reaches its climax on the last Sunday of the Church Year and the first Sundays of Advent) is frightening to the serious-minded follower of Christ. We cannot avoid asking ourselves: Does Christ now dwell by faith in our hearts? Are we rooted and grounded in charity? Are we filled unto all the fullness of God?

No one can answer those questions with full assurance. But we can all pray: "Have mercy on me, O Lord, for I have cried to Thee all the day; for Thou, O Lord, art sweet and mild, and plenteous in mercy to all that call upon Thee. Bow down Thy ear to me, O Lord, and hear me; for I am needy and poor" (Introit). And then we can go on to one of the most compact, most theological, of all the prayers in the missal: "Let Thy grace, we beg of Thee, O Lord, *ever precede and follow us*, and may it stir up a never-failing zeal for good works" (Collect); for our experience in life, and especially our

243

acquaintance with our personal weaknesses, has finally convinced us that we depend on God's grace for everything. We need it to begin a good action, to carry it through, and to follow it up. He alone "is able to do all those things more abundantly than we desire or understand, in keeping with the power that is at work in us" (Epistle). God is and always will be the great Worker of holiness in man, a fact that today's Gospel again wonderfully demonstrates.

HE WHO HUMBLES HIMSELF

"Is it lawful to heal on the Sabbath?" our Lord asked (Gospel). But the Pharisees remained silent. So Jesus took the sick man, healed him, and let him go. "Which of you shall have an ass or an ox fall into a pit, and will not immediately draw him up on the Sabbath?" Today we are in Christ's house. We are the man sick with spiritual dropsy. Christ loves us with the tenderest, most merciful love. We mean more to Him than an ox or an ass could ever mean to any owner. There is no question in His mind about it being lawful to heal us on the Sabbath. It is His weekly privilege. But to heal us permanently, to help us unto progress of the inner man so that we may eventually be filled unto all the fullness of God, He requires some cooperation from us.

And so He says to us: "When thou art invited to a wedding feast, do not recline in the first place... But when thou art invited, go and recline in the last place... For everyone who exalts himself shall be humbled, and he who humbles himself shall be exalted" (Gospel). The cooperation He requires from us is humility, the frank admission that we are sinners, and the conviction that we need Him and His grace always.

"Look down, O Lord, to help me; let them be confounded and ashamed that seek after my soul to take it away; look down, O Lord, to help me" (Offertory verse). Such is the prayer of the humble man. But it is useless unless it is followed by the action that best suits a humble man, namely, sacrificial action. The gifts lie upon the altar. But bread and wine on the altar offered in our name mean that we lie there: our lives, present and future, our worry and our work, even our defects and failures. "Cleanse us, we implore Thee, O Lord, by the effect of the sacrifice here present, and in Thy mercy make us worthy to share in it" (Secret).

May you be strengthened with power through His Spirit unto the progress of the inner man; may Christ dwell in your hearts... in order that you may be filled unto all the fullness of God. The grace of God that ever precedes and follows us, stirring up zeal for good works is the grace to be sincere, honest, and humble in our sacrifice. Through it we arrive at progress of the inner man unto all the fullness of God. Through it we prepare ourselves for the Judgment. And because by humble sacrifice we have opened our hearts to God, He fills us with the confidence that makes us cry out: "O Lord, I will be mindful of Thy justice alone: Thou hast taught me, O God, from my youth, and unto old age and gray hairs, O God, forsake me not" (Communion verse).

The Lord has done and can do wonderful things (Alleluia verse). "To Him be glory in the Church and in

Christ Jesus down through all the ages of time without end. Amen" (Epistle).

FOOD FOR THE WAY

1. Have mercy on me, O Lord, for I have cried to Thee all the day; for Thou, O Lord, art sweet and mild, and plenteous in mercy to all that call upon Thee (Introit).

2. Sing ye to the Lord a new canticle, because the Lord hath done wonderful things (Alleluia verse).

3. Everyone who exalts himself shall be humbled, and he who humbles himself shall be exalted (Gospel).

SEVENTEENTH SUNDAY AFTER PENTECOST

WHAT DO YOU THINK OF CHRIST ?

It is possible to take Christ too much for granted, but not if we make the spirit of these Sunday Masses our own. The texts of the Masses keep our thinking about Christ and God in line with primitive sources, namely, with the mind of God Himself.

Today our Lord Himself is our instructor. "What do you think of the Christ?" He asks the Pharisees (and us). "Whose son is He?" He is David's son, they answer. But our Lord comes right back at them: "How then does David in the Spirit call Him Lord....? If David calls him 'Lord,' how is he his son?" And no one could answer him a word (Gospel).

The implication is clear: Christ is *God's* Son. This Jesus who has chosen us to be His followers and apostles, who has made us to share His Life in Baptism as an engrafted branch shares in the life of the tree-trunk, who has made us members of Himself and of one another in a holy community, who heals us in His sacraments and feeds us with His Body and Blood, who worships with us at every Mass, who speaks to us in every

Gospel — this Jesus is *Man*. But by His word "the heavens were established; and all the power of them by the spirit of His mouth" (Gradual). Therefore He is also *God*. He will come again to judge the living and the dead.

THE WAY OF THE LORD

He is our Creator, our Lord and Master. We owe Him humble adoration and respectful reverence. "To the Lord your God let your vows be made and paid... to God that is feared among all the kings of the earth" (Communion verse, Knox translation). But we are not mere slaves prostrate in the dirt before Him. He wants more from us than blind, fear-motivated service. And it was in order that He would get more than fear from us that He gave us our freedom. We can choose to serve Him with thanksgiving and praise motivated by love.

But the freedom that He gave us — blessed gift though it is — can also be the occasion of our downfall. Because of it we can sin, we can refuse to love. And so today, faced with the awe-inducing picture of the glorified Christ who is soon to come in glory to judge us, our first thought is of our unworthiness and sinfulness. Therefore we pray: "Grant to Thy people, we pray Thee, O Lord, to avoid every contact with the devil and with a pure mind to follow only Thee (Collect).

We shall have to give an account of our stewardship to Him. "Thou art just, O Lord, and Thy judgment is right." But He is also our Father. Our Lord has told us that. Therefore, "Deal with Thy servant according to Thy mercy" (Introit). He has always been merciful to

248

us, and He will be unto the end. The proof is in today's Epistle. But meanwhile, through St. Paul, He asks us to use our gift of freedom and "to walk in a manner worthy of the calling with which you were called" (Epistle).

He has called us to union with Him, to allowing ourselves to be filled unto all the fullness of God (remember last Sunday's Epistle). But He has also called us to union with our brethren. Therefore we must "with all humility and meekness, with patience, bear with one another in love, careful to preserve the unity of the Spirit in the bond of peace: one body and one Spirit, even as you were called in one hope of your calling; one Lord, one faith, one Baptism; one God and Father of all, who is above all, and throughout all, and in us all, who is blessed forever. Amen" (Epistle).

THOU SHALT LOVE

"Blessed are the undefiled in the way, *who walk in the law of the Lord*" (Introit). We are one with God, and one with one another. There is only one way in which we can walk worthy of that vocation: "Thou shalt love the Lord thy God with thy whole heart, and with thy whole soul, and with thy whole mind" (Gospel). Love is the gift of self to the beloved. It is union of minds and wills. We love God when we give ourselves to Him in such a way that, having emptied our hearts of self-love, God can fill them with Himself.

Such love purifies, saves, gives joy and peace. But when we give ourselves to God, when we identify our minds and hearts with His mind and His heart, it follows necessarily that we must love those whom God loves, our neighbors. Love of God is the greatest and the first commandment. "And the second is like to it, 'Thou shalt love thy neighbor as thyself.'" If love for God demands the gift of self to Him, it also demands the gift of self to all who belong to Him in His blessed community; and more than that, it demands the gift of self to those outside that community. It is gift of self to these that will win them over.

Thus the apostolate assumes the nature of God's own relation to us. His love for us prompted the giving of Himself to us in the Incarnation. By that gift He wants to woo and win our loving service. By our gift of self to our fellowmen God through us desires to woo and win others to Himself and to His community.

Blessed is the nation whose God is the Lord: the people whom He hath chosen for His inheritance" (Gradual). We believe firmly that Christ is the Lord of the Universe, the supreme Judge of all. We worship Him in all awe and reverence. But He who is above all and throughout all, is also in us all. He is God-with-us and God-with-our-brethren. This is our answer to Christ's question, "What do you think of the Christ?"

FOOD FOR THE WAY

1. O Lord, hear my prayer; and let my cry come to Thee (Alleluia verse).
2. Walk in a manner worthy of the vocation with which you were called (Epistle).
3. Favorably look down upon this people upon whom Thy Name is invoked (Offertory verse).

250

EIGHTEENTH SUNDAY AFTER PENTECOST

GIVE PEACE, O LORD

God is infinite Life, boundless Love. He stamps every soul that comes forth from His creating hand with a deep and powerful urge to return to Him to be filled with that Life and that Love. Hearts made for union with the Infinite must ever remain restless if we try to satisfy them with anything less than the Infinite. The traveller's homesickness, the sufferer's cry for release from pain, everyman's thirst for relaxation and change, and all other longings are but small-scale expressions of the restlessness of the human heart engaged in its fundamental yearning for God.

The Liturgical Year is drawing to its close; another one is gradually announcing itself. A new theme has been evident the last few Sundays. There is no longer any doubt: the theme of Advent — *the return of our Lord* at Christmas and at the end of time — fills these Sunday Masses. We are awaiting the appearance of our Lord Jesus Christ, "who will strengthen our resolution to the last so that no charge will lie against us on the day when our Lord Jesus Christ comes (Epistle, Knox translation).

It is autumn, the time of harvest, the time for gathering in the fruits of the trees, the grain from the fields. Harvest inevitably reminds us of God's harvest time, and we can be pardoned if we are a little uneasy about that. At our Baptism Christ planted us in His garden, the Church. Another year of our earthly life is almost gone. "By their fruits you shall know them." But what are our fruits? What advance have we made this year in union with God and with one another?

Perhaps we have tried to fill our hearts with the fluffy meringue of material excitement. And now finally our hearts rebell. It was inevitable that the old, basic, demanding desire for true peace and joy and for final union with God should assert itself. "Give peace, O Lord, to them that patiently wait for Thee... Hear the prayers of Thy servant, and of Thy people Israel" (Introit).

BE OF GOOD HEART

Give peace, O Lord... Peace, we need it, we were made for it, we must have it. God would not give us a thirst which He could not or would not satisfy. But how can we rise up to greet Christ at His return and receive our fill of God when our sins have deadened our desire for Him and have laid us low on a bed of spiritual paralysis like the man in today's Gospel?

Christ Himself answers us: "Take courage, son; thy sins are forgiven thee." The same Christ who forgave the sins of the sick man and healed his body to prove that He had the power to forgive sins passed on that very same power to His Church. In this very Mass, and each time we go to confession, the Christ of the Gospel appears to us. His Sacrifice on Calvary and the Life-giving effects of that Sacrifice penetrate our souls. "Take courage, son, thy sins are forgiven thee. Arise, take up thy bed, and go into thy house." There will come a day when He will repeat that command once and for all. Only then He will substitute "heaven" for "house."

By His death, Christ opens for us the way to God who draws us to Himself. More than that, He fits us out for union with God by joining us to Himself at Baptism. After Baptism He forgives our sins in holy Penance. And, as though that were not enough, "by means of the communion in this adorable Sacrifice He *makes us partakers of the Supreme Godhead*" (Secret). Indeed, "in everything we have been enriched in him... so that we lack no grace, while awaiting the appearance of our Lord Jesus Christ" (Epistle).

THE FRUIT OF SACRIFICE

"Our hearts are restless till they rest in Thee." But our hearts do rest in God when we share fully in His holy Sacrifice. Then they are at peace. However, if our hunger for God is not satisfied at Mass, then perhaps the second part of the Secret prayer gives the reason:

"Grant, we pray Thee, that since we know Thy truth (about our being made partakers of the Godhead), we may live up to it by a worthy life." We must want the answer to that prayer and do our best to cooperate with His willingness to help us to our dignity.

Religion is not mere emotional desire. We thirst for God. Nothing on earth can fully satisfy us, nothing, that is, except Holy Mass. But even the Mass will not help unless we learn to sacrifice ourselves in it. "Not everyone who says to me, 'Lord, Lord,' shall enter the kingdom of heaven; but he that does the will of My Father in heaven shall enter the kingdom of heaven" (Matthew 7:21). Therefore, we must "bring up sacrifices (of our hearts and entire beings) and come into His courts and adore the Lord in His holy court" (Communion verse).

The one who said that "Peace is the fruit of sacrifice" was right, because the fruit of the Sacrifice of the Mass is the Prince of Peace, the Lamb of God, the Victim of Calvary, with whom through Holy Communion we become one. "*He* is our peace" (Ephesians 2:14). He will strengthen our resolution to the last, so that no charge will lie against us on the day when our Lord Jesus Christ comes.

Christ is coming in judgment. "The Gentiles shall fear Thy Name, O Lord: and all the kings of the earth Thy glory" (Alleluia verse). But Sacrifice will have destroyed *our* fear even as it will have sharpened our desire. And so we shall be able to say with full and grateful hearts: "I rejoiced at the things that were said to me: WE SHALL GO INTO THE HOUSE OF THE LORD" (Gradual).

FOOD FOR THE WAY

1. Give peace, O Lord, to them that patiently wait for Thee... hear the prayers of Thy people Israel (Introit).

2. Take courage, son; thy sins are forgiven thee (Gospel).

3. Bring up sacrifices, and come into His courts: adore ye the Lord in His holy court (Communion verse).

NINETEENTH SUNDAY AFTER PENTECOST

THE WEDDING FEAST

"The kingdom of heaven is like a king who made a marriage feast for his son" (Gospel). The King is God the Father. The Son is Jesus Christ. The marriage took place when the Son of God took our human nature as His bride. The results of that union were divine Life and Love, and a divine way of living made available for all mankind.

Christ's Father in heaven insists that the invited guests come to the feast. "And he sent his servants to call those invited to the marriage feast, but they would not come." They had a great variety of excuses, and they made light of the invitation. Some went off, one to his farm, and another to his business; and the rest lay hold of the king's servants, treated them shamefully, and even killed them. Finally, after all manner of arguments were used, the wedding feast was filled with guests. The king came in to see the guests and found one of them without a wedding garment. "Bind his hands and feet," the king commanded, "and cast him forth into the darkness outside, where there will be weeping and gnashing of teeth."

We were fortunate enough to receive invitations to this blessed marriage feast. We entered into the joy of the banquet hall at our Baptism. The joy, the Life, the Spirit of Christ the Bridegroom possessed us; we had actually "put on Christ" (Galatians 3:27). Our wedding garment of divine Grace was spotless and new. But then our life in the world began; and things have not been going so well. By associating too frequently with those who want nothing to do with Christ and allowing ourselves to become infected with their lack of interest in Him, we have allowed our wedding garment to grow worn and flimsy. Perhaps we have even lost it altogether. That loss makes us all the more unhappy; for it is only at the Wedding Feast that our desires can be satisfied. There is always a close connection between our moral life and our happiness.

What is more, the time is drawing near when the King is going to return to look over the guests. He may have to say to us: "Friend, how didst thou come in here without a wedding garment?" We know in our hearts that we can have no good answer to that question. Once in the Church, there is no excuse for not having the wedding garment of baptismal grace clean and brightly shining all the time.

SALVATION OF THE PEOPLE

There can be no excuse, because Christ is constantly working on us and in us. During every Liturgical Year

He renews our baptismal life of grace. In fact He does it at every Mass. Holy Mass is the feast that renews and reenacts the eternal Feast of our Redemption. At every Mass Christ stands before us guests as He did on Calvary and says to us: "I am the salvation of the people: in whatever tribulation they shall cry to Me, I will hear them, and I will be their Lord forever" (Introit).

We are to take His words literally. Whatever may be our spiritual state, if we cry to Him, He will hear us. But He does lay down one condition: "Attend, O my people, to My law: incline your ears to the words of my mouth" (Introit). Then He tells us what His law is: "Put away lying and speak truth each one with his neighbor, because *we are members one of another...* do not let the sun go down upon your anger: do not give place to the devil. He who was wont to steal, let him steal no longer; but rather let him labor, working with his hands at what is good, that he may have something to share with him who suffers need" (Epistle). If we try to observe this law and incline our ears to the words of His mouth, i.e. His year-long prayer of praise and glorification of the Father, we need have no fear of a dirty, shapeless wedding garment when the King comes to inspect.

Our wedding garment is truly clean only when we are "renewed in the spirit of our mind, when we have put on the new man, which was created according to God in justice and holiness of truth" (Epistle). The new man, which Christ wants us to be, has the mind of Christ. He is charitable to all, just, sympathetic, upright.

258

Above all, he is desirous of furthering with all his might the will of the King that more and more guests be brought into the wedding feast so that the banquet hall may be filled.

MEDICINAL OPERATION

But Christ's telling us what to do would avail us little if we did not have the strength to carry out His suggestions and to do His will. He takes care of that too... at Holy Mass. In the variable parts of the Mass He carefully builds up in our minds and hearts a longing to be one with our God. He fills us with consciousness of our sinfulness; He praises God with us; He feeds us with life-giving truth.

Then at the offertory, He gives us the opportunity to purge out our sinful self-will, the commonest source of spiritual disease. There and at the Consecration we enter into His death, but death is swallowed up in victory. "If I shall walk in the midst of tribulation, Thou wilt quicken me, O Lord" (Offertory verse). Finally, at Holy Communion (which the Postcommunion prayer calls a "medicinalis operation," a "healing operation") we receive the Body and Blood of Jesus Christ. This divine Medicine rids us of all "wickedness of heart," it repairs damages, it is the primary and indispensable source of permanent spiritual health and well-being. No, there is no excuse for us ever to be without a wedding garment that is spotless, clean, and shining.

FOOD FOR THE WAY

1. Let my prayer be directed as incense in Thy sight, O Lord. The lifting up of my hands as evening sacrifice (Gradual).

2. Friend, how didst thou come in here without a wedding garment (Gospel)?

3. Thou hast commanded Thy commandments to be kept most diligently: O that my ways may be directed to keep Thy justifications (Communion verse).

TWENTIETH SUNDAY AFTER PENTECOST

THE RIVERS OF BABYLON

To receive full benefit from this Mass we must recall what was in the minds of the Jewish victims of the Babylonian Captivity of about 586 B.C. "Upon the rivers of Babylon, there we sat and wept; when we remembered Thee, O Sion (Offertory verse). The Jews in exile are types of all of us Christians exiled in our earthly Babylon. As they longed to return to Jerusalem, so should we in our pilgrim-life here below yearn for lasting union with God in our heavenly Sion.

The time of our deliverance is not far off. We long for it, but at the same time we fear that we may not yet be ready for it. Like the son of the certain royal official of today's Gospel, we lie in bed sick with a fever. Our fever is sin and ungodly attachment to the material attractions of our land of exile. We still love sin, much as we suffer from its hold on us, with a passion that could well endanger our release from exile and our happy return to our true home.

But there is still time. When the sick boy's father

261

"heard that Jesus had come into Galilee, he went to him and besought him to come down and heal his son, for he was at the point of death. 'Sir, come down before my child dies.' Jesus said to him, 'Go thy way, thy son lives'" (Gospel). Jesus is in the Galilee of our churches today. To us He says, "Go thy way, thy son lives." But His cure will be effective and lasting only on condition that we fulfill certain prescriptions of today's Mass.

REDEEMING THE TIME

We must first of all be aware of the nature of our sickness. "All that Thou hast done to us, O Lord, Thou hast done in true judgment; *because we have sinned against Thee, and we have not obeyed Thy commandments*" (Introit). Each of us can fill in for himself the details and the enumeration of the disobedience of God's commandments that has brought on our sickness. It is right that we should take the consequences of our having forsaken our God. But then if God's being just glorifies Him, is He not even more glorified by being merciful to us? "Give glory to Thy Name, and deal with us according to the multitude of Thy mercy" (Introit). "Be appeased, O generous God, and to Thy faithful people grant peace and pardon, so that after being cleansed from all their sins, they may serve Thee with a secure mind" (Collect).

How we are to serve God with secure minds in this exile of ours is revealed to us in one of the most exalted Epistles of the whole year: "Brethren: see to it that you walk with care: not as unwise, but as wise, making the most of your time (the old translation had it "redeeming the time") because the days are evil. Therefore do not become foolish, but *understand what the will of the Lord is*. And do not be drunk with wine, for in that is debauchery." Again we are brought face to face with essentials: understand what the will of the Lord is and then live according to that will. Our exile is painful. But there is nothing to be gained in seeking to forget the exile by the escapist device of too much drinking or other excesses. Such over-indulgence brings on that unpleasant condition called a hangover, which is just the physical counterpart of the even more unpleasant hangover in our conscience. We wake up and the exile is still there, and added to our longing for God is a disgust with ourselves for having been "unwise in not redeeming the time."

There is only one kind of inebriation whereby we can understand what God's will is for us: "Be filled with the *Holy Spirit*, speaking to one another in psalms and hymns and spiritual songs, singing and making melody in your hearts to the Lord, giving thanks always for all things in the name of our Lord Jesus Christ to God the Father" (Epistle). St. Paul must have smiled as he wrote those words comparing inebriation brought on by the Holy Spirit and that induced by the ordinary kind of "spirits." He knew that being filled with the Holy Spirit, we glow and sparkle with the warm knowledge that God is our Father, just but also merciful, that we are on our way home to Him, that He loves us and wants to help us get there. We are expansive and friendly with our neighbor and want them to join us in our common songs of praise to God. We have no fear of the last (or any) day, because the Holy Spirit who fills us knows no fear, but only love.

MEAT IN DUE SEASON

We are in exile, but the exile of the faithful follower of Christ differs considerably from that of the man who does not even know that he is homesick. We are not alone. Christ our God has come to us, dwells among us, and heals our wounds with a "heavenly medicine that roots out all vice from our hearts" (Secret), and replaces the vice with the pardon and peace that is already now a beginning of eternal joy.

It is Christ who at Holy Mass is constantly filling us with the Holy Spirit; for the Spirit it is who remains with us as the most blessed result of our participation in Mass and Communion. "The eyes of all hope in Thee, O Lord; and Thou givest them meat in due season. Thou openest Thy hand, and fillest every living creature with blessing" (Gradual).

But not even the Holy Spirit can help us, "inebriate" us, and make us want to sing out our happiness unless we are continually aware with a living faith of His exciting presence within us. This awareness can come only by daily cultivation and effort, in a word, by mental prayer. And if we want to know what mental prayer is and how to go about it, the Church tells us in this Mass. All we need to do is to obey the Alleluia verse. "My heart is ready, O God, my heart is ready: I will sing, and will give praise to Thee, my glory."

A heart ready for God will have God. It will sing

and praise Him. It will fear no evil. It will no longer weep at being exiled, because its exile is already over; for it is able to say: "Be Thou mindful of Thy word to Thy servant, O Lord, in which Thou hast given me hope: this hath comforted me in my humiliation" (Communion verse).

FOOD FOR THE WAY

1. Blessed are the undefiled in the way; who walk in the law of the Lord (Introit).

2. The eyes of all hope in Thee, O Lord; and Thou givest them meat in due season (Gradual).

3. Upon the rivers of Babylon, there we sat and wept; when we remembered Thee, O Sion (Offertory verse).

TWENTY-FIRST SUNDAY
AFTER PENTECOST

SETTLING ACCOUNTS

"The kingdom of heaven is likened to a king who desired to settle accounts with his servants" (Gospel). The king is God: eternal, almighty, supreme. "All things are in Thy will, O Lord ("at Thy disposal," says Mgr. Knox); and there is none that can resist Thy will: for Thou hast made all things, heaven and earth, and all things that are under the cope of heaven: THOU ART THE LORD OF ALL" (Introit).

The end is coming closer and closer — the end of this Liturgical Year that foreshadows the end of our life, the end of our world. The King desires to settle accounts. There is no escaping that day of reckoning. Today's Mass shows how two men prepared to meet their eternal judge.

The one man is described by our Lord in the Gospel. He is the wicked servant who would not forgive his fellow servant a *little* debt in spite of the fact that his master had just forgiven him a very *great* debt. His mind was fixed on material riches as being more precious than honor, charity, and the unity of friendship with

266

his fellowmen. It would be hard to improve on this short but cutting portrait of a small-minded, selfish, worldly, avaricious candidate for the title of the world's meanest man. And all will agree that he received what was coming to him: " 'Wicked servant! I forgave thee all the debt, because thou didst entreat me. Shouldst not thou also have had pity on thy fellow servant, even as I had pity on thee?' And his master, being angry, handed him over to the torturers until he should pay all that was due him" (Gospel).

THE MAN IN THE LAND OF HUS

The other portrait the Church shows us is that of Job, "the man in the land of Hus, simple, and upright, and fearing God" (Offertory verse). God allowed Satan to tempt Job, and no one will deny that the devil was most thorough in his mischief: 'He (Satan) destroyed all his substance and his children; and wounded his flesh also with a grievous ulcer."

But Job's thinking was right. He was simple, upright, and he feared God. For Him God was everything, the "Lord of All," who could take away even as He had first given. For Job knew that "Before the mountains were made, or the earth and the world was formed; *from eternity and to eternity Thou art God*" (Gradual). But he also knew that God was his father, and therefore no misfortune could dislodge the hand of trust and love with which he held on to God. "My soul is in Thy salvation and in Thy word have I hoped: when wilt Thou execute judgment on them that per-

secute me? the wicked have persecuted me: help me,
O Lord my God" (Communion verse). There are few
men in biblical history who measured everything —
their lives, possessions, and loved ones — so exactly
according to the yardstick of God's supremacy and
mercy. And therefore there were few if any who were as
well prepared as he to settle accounts with his King.

IF YOU DO NOT FORGIVE

The King desires to settle accounts with all his
servants. We have a choice. We can be like the wicked
servant, or we can be like Job. "Blessed are the undefiled in the way; who walk in the law of the Lord"
(Introit). This is the third time in these late after-
Pentecost Masses that our life's ideal has thus been
worded for us. We are to be undefiled in the way of our
life; we are to walk in the law of the Lord. We were
told in the last Easter season to keep ourselves unspotted
from this world (Epistle, Fifth Sunday after Easter).
And we have been told again and again that the Law
of the Lord is love for God and for our neighbor and
abandonment to His holy will.

But here we are facing the end; and sober reflection
reveals an annoying resemblance between each of us
and the wicked servant rather than with Job. God is
love. And those who would enter paradise must have
hearts made capable of sharing infinite Love by prac-
ticing love for and forgiveness of neighbors in this life.
All through the year these Sunday Masses have imposed this love upon us. Perhaps now at the end we

begin to realize how necessary it is... and how imperfect we have been in cultivating it. The wicked and unforgiving servant was handed over to the torturers until he paid all the debt. "So also my heavenly Father will do to you, if you do not each forgive your brothers from your hearts" (Gospel).

We might well depart from this Mass in depressed spirits were it not for St. Paul, that sturdy enemy of faintheartedness. He knew what a cross life can be. And the prospect of the imminent return of Christ in judgment was more real to him and his Christians than it is to us.

The struggle is hard and the odds against us are heavy (Principalities and Powers, the world-rulers of this darkness, the spiritual forces of wickedness on high, not to mention our own too easy tendencies to give in to the demands of our animal appetites). But, he tells us, "Be strengthened in the Lord and in the might of His power. Put on the armor of God, that you may be able to stand against the wiles of the devil... that you may be able to resist in the evil day... Stand, therefore, having girded your loins with truth, and having put on the breast-plate of justice, and having your feet shod with the readiness of the gospel of peace, in all things taking up the shield of faith, with which you may be able to quench all the fiery darts of the most wicked one. And take unto you the helmet of salvation and the sword of the spirit, that is, the word of God" (Epistle).

The armor of God, the breast-plate of justice, the gospel of peace, the shield of faith, the sword of the spirit, the word of God — all these things have been available to us throughout this Liturgical Year. Truly, the Lord has "been our refuge from generation to generation" (Gradual). But we have to take these things and put them on. God cannot do everything for us. What Job could do, we can do, especially "after being nourished with the food of immortality" (Postcommunion prayer), whereby God Himself becomes our shield and our strength.

THOU ART THE LORD OF ALL. Help us to be simple, and upright, and fearing God.

FOOD FOR THE WAY

1. All things are in Thy will, O Lord: and there is none that can resist Thy will: for Thou hast made all things... Thou art the Lord of all (Introit)!

2. So also my heavenly Father will do to you, if you do not each forgive your brothers from your hearts (Gospel).

3. The wicked have persecuted me: help me, O Lord my God (Communion verse)!

TWENTY-SECOND SUNDAY AFTER PENTECOST

THE DAY OF CHRIST

In the spiritual life there is danger at times that we think too much in terms of our own efforts. For example, we may have been considering these last eleven months of following Christ in the Liturgical Year unto our growth in union with Him as our work exclusively. And that may be the cause for our worry these late Sundays about our general lack of preparedness for the coming of the "day of Christ" (Epistle). Man's work is bound to be imperfect.

It is right that we should be concerned about the last day. But one fact we must not forget is that this Liturgy is the Lord's work (we said that already last Advent), and it is a powerful, divine work. In today's Epistle St. Paul gives our thinking on the subject the correct slant: "I am convinced in the Lord Jesus that *he who has begun a good work in you will bring it to perfection until the day of Christ Jesus.*" Therefore, our spiritual development during this year has been first of all the work-

271

ing of Christ within us. It is He who is "our refuge and our strength and the source of all devotion" (Collect).

Our part is to have a great joy in collaborating with Him who has begun the work in us and who will do everything in His power to carry it through. "They that fear the Lord, *let them hope in Him: He is their helper and protector*" (Alleluia verse). It is He who works within us to give us the boldness to "argue" with God: "If Thou shalt observe iniquities, O Lord, Lord, who shall endure it" (Introit)? But it is He also who tempers our boldness with the certain knowledge of our helplessness without Him, our utter need for Him: "With Thee is propitiation, O God of Israel. From the depths I have cried to Thee, O Lord: Lord, hear my voice" (Introit).

THE THINGS THAT ARE GOD'S

Finally it is Christ who gives us the device whereby we can help Him to complete the good work He has begun in us and thus assist us to prepare ourselves for judgment.

Christ's enemies, seeking to trap Him, ask if it is lawful to pay tribute to Caesar. Jesus asks for the coin of the tribute. " 'Whose are this image and inscription?' They said to him, 'Caesar's.' Then he said to them, 'RENDER, THEREFORE, TO CAESAR THE THINGS THAT ARE CAESAR'S, AND TO GOD THE THINGS THAT ARE GOD'S' " (Gospel).

We have here the most basic bit of advice in the spiritual life. According to Father Parsch, Christ is simply telling us that the best preparation for Judgment

272

Day is the perfect accomplishment of the duties of our state of life, whatever it might be. Render to Caesar... Render to God.

We must be clear about our Lord's full meaning. First of all, He does not mean that our religious life, our service of God, should be separated from our life in civil society. Nor does He intend that prayers and spiritual exercises can do away with the necessity of performing well the requirements of our particular state of life. For example, it would be wrong for a mother to neglect her family in order to give herself to individual prayers. Religious exercises will not absolve a student from the duty of study that is imposed on him by his vocation as a student.

What our Lord does want is that there be no divorce between our religious life and our everyday duties as workers, students, husbands, wives, farmers, business and professional men and women. Whatever we do as members of Christ, if done well and from a general motive of love for God, *is service of God*. It is divine worship. It glorifies God. It helps to sanctify us... and others. Render to God the things that are God's implies that we are to become saints and thus prepare for the day of Christ in and through, and not in spite of, our particular God-given vocation.

"Whose are this image and inscription?" our Lord asks. He could ask the same thing about us. Whose image and inscription are stamped on us? Just as the civic ruler's image is stamped on a coin, so is God's image stamped on us at our Baptism and Confirmation. We belong to Him and to His work. Hence we must "render to God the things that are God's." All that we are, all that we do, we must give to Him. But there are so many of our fellow-citizens who are not so sealed with His image, His baptismal character. These also we must do our best to give Him; for they also belong to Him.

DWELLING TOGETHER IN UNITY

Our rendering to God the things that are God's is to be a community affair. We are to go to Him, not so much as individuals, but as members one of another. "Behold how good and how pleasant it is for brethren to dwell together in unity" (Gradual). In these Sunday Masses Christ and His Church think always in terms of the community. "Give ear to the devout prayers of Thy *Church*, and grant that what *we* ask in faith *we* may obtain in fact" (Collect). "Grant unto *us*, O God of mercy, that this saving sacrifice may forever free *us* from our guilty deeds, and shield *us* from all harm" (Secret).

"Master, we know that thou art truthful, and that thou teachest the way of God in truth and that thou carest naught for any man; for thou dost not regard the person of men" (Gospel). The enemies of Christ said that with their tongues in their mouths. We say it with full knowledge that it is God's own truth. Christ has the way of life. Render to Caesar: render to God. Rendering to God the things that are God's is therefore best fulfilled by our striving to complete, to perfect, to consecrate the being and the doing of the Christian community — the parish, the family, the school, the nation. And it is to that end that St. Paul prays today: "That *your charity may more and more abound* in knowledge

274

and all discernment, so that you may approve the better things, that you may be upright and without offense *unto the day of Christ*, filled with the fruit of justice, through Jesus Christ, to the glory and praise of God" (Epistle).

FOOD FOR THE WAY

1. From the depths I have cried to Thee, O Lord; Lord, hear my voice (Introit).

2. Remember me, O Lord, Thou Who rulest above all power (Offertory verse).

3. I have cried, for Thou, O God, hast heard me: O incline Thy ear unto me, and hear my words (Communion verse).

TWENTY-THIRD SUNDAY
AFTER PENTECOST

THE TASSEL OF CHRIST'S CLOAK

The Gospel of this Mass tells about a woman who, after suffering from a hemorrhage for twelve years was finally healed by merely touching the tassels of our Lord's cloak. "If I touch but his cloak I shall be saved," she said to herself. "But Jesus, turning and seeing her, said, 'Take courage, daughter; thy faith has saved thee.' And the woman was restored to health from that moment" (Gospel).

This is an excellent example of what the Liturgy can do to us. Our wide-awake, loving participation in these Sunday Masses is our holding out our hands to touch Christ's garments which are the texts of these Masses. In St. Luke's account of the same incident our Lord is reported as asking: "Who touched me? Someone touched me; for I perceived that *power had gone forth from me*" (Luke 8:46). He can say the same about us at every Mass. Power, health, new Life, comes forth from Christ to us. "Take courage, thy faith has saved thee."

276

THOUGHTS OF PEACE

The garments of Christ today are full of new inspiration and courage for those of us who hold out their hands with faith to touch them. There is first of all the confidence, the quiet assurance, that fills us as we hear the voice of God our Father upon our entrance into our churches: "I think thoughts of peace, and not of affliction: you shall call upon Me, and I will hear you" (Introit).

For years we have been suffering from all manner of diseases, spiritual and physical. Now we face death and judgment. But here is our God telling us that He loves us with an everlasting love, that His thinking about us is merciful and forgiving, that He is not intent upon our destruction but rather our rescue from eternal death. He knows our weaknesses, but if from the depths of our lowliness and misery we cry out to Him, He will hear our prayer (Offertory verse) and will bring us back from the captive exile of our life in this world into the joy of eternal union with Him. There is gratitude and joy, therefore, in our appreciation of these facts: "Thou hast delivered us, O Lord, from them that afflict us: and hast put them to shame that hate us. In God we will glory all the day: and in Thy Name we will praise forever" (Gradual).

THE WARNING

But we must hold tight to those garments of Christ. There are some Christians — perhaps we have been among them — "who are enemies of the cross of Christ. Their end is ruin, their God is their belly, their glory is in their shame, they mind the things of earth" (Epistle). Thus does our Lord warn us, and in this He shows His love for us just as much as in His encouragement at the beginning of the Mass.

To be an enemy of the cross of Christ, that cross which is a saving cross for us and our world! That is possible. The Catholic who makes his belly his god, who clings to the things of earth to the degree that they command all his love and attention, who is unapostolic and uninterested in his vocation to be Christ to his fellowmen — that man's end is ruin, ruin for himself and for those whom he has failed to bring to Christ. God's thought of peace will have a hard time competing with the will to destroy himself of this enemy of His Son's cross. Hence the appropriateness of our prayer today: "O Lord, we beg of Thee, absolve the sins of Thy people, so that by Thy kind forgiveness we may be set free from the chains of our sins in which our weakness had entangled us."

HEAVENLY CITIZENSHIP

But we will have our hand on our Lord's garments. "Take courage," He says to us, and be imitators of St. Paul, My voice, My apostle. This is what St. Paul tells us: "Our citizenship is in heaven from which also we eagerly await a Savior, our Lord Jesus Christ" (Epistle). After we have suffered a little while, after we have spent ourselves in bringing other sufferers to Christ and to a realization of the fact that their citizenship is also in heaven, our Lord "will refashion the body of our lowliness, conforming it to the body of his glory by exerting the power by which he is also able to subject all things to Himself" (Epistle).

"I believe in the resurrection of the body and life everlasting," we say in the Apostles' Creed. On the last day these bodies of ours will rise again glorified to be joined forever with our souls. It is man, the whole of him — soul and body — whom Christ has redeemed.

Christ is even now working at that transformation of our bodies and fitting them for the resurrection through the Eucharist. Power went out from Christ to the woman, and she was restored to health simply by touching his garment. But He Himself comes to us in the Eucharist to be our food, our health, our resurrection. In the Eucharist He "gladdens us with a share of divine life" (Postcommunion prayer). In the Eucharist we offer the sacrifice of praise for the sake of increasing our service and of completing in us What He mercifully began without any merit of ours (Secret prayer) when He first gave Himself to us in Baptism. The Eucharist, as we mentioned once before, is the seed of glory.

"If I touch but his cloak I shall be saved." Judgment is coming. But we are unafraid. We do not fear because we have Christ, the same Christ who healed the woman with the hemorrhage, who brought back the ruler's daughter to life (Gospel). This Christ tells us: "All things whatever you ask for in prayer, believe that you shall receive, and they shall come to you" (Communion prayer). From the depths we cry out to Him to hear us, to rescue us, to save us from death. And this is His answer. *All things whatever* you ask for they shall come to you. Truly, "Lord, Thou hast blessed Thy land, Thou hast turned away the captivity of Jacob" (Introit). In God we will glory all the day.

FOOD FOR THE WAY

1. I think thoughts of peace, and not of affliction (Introit).

2. Our citizenship is in heaven from which also we eagerly await a savior, our Lord Jesus Christ (Epistle).

3. Take courage, daughter; thy faith has saved thee (Gospel).

TWENTY-FOURTH SUNDAY
AFTER PENTECOST

(Fifth After Epiphany)

NOTE: "If there are more than twenty-four Sundays after Pentecost, the Introit, Gradual, Alleluia, Offertory, and Communion verses of the twenty-third Sunday are repeated on all the remaining Sundays. But the Collects, Epistle, and Gospel are taken from those Sundays that were passed over after the Epiphany" (St. Andrew's Missal).

. . . .

WHEAT AND WEEDS

Today's Mass paints two portraits of the Church (and of any Christian community that is the Church in miniature — parish, school, family). The one, by Christ, is the Church as it is, with the weeds growing alongside of the good grain and with weeds and wheat together daily approaching final harvest. "The kingdom of heaven is like a man who sowed good seed in his field;

but... his enemy came and sowed weeds among the wheat, and went away" (Gospel).

We may well wonder about the problem of evil and ask ourselves why God allows it. Why does He not "remove" evil men and environments before they have a chance to corrupt others and thus make Christian living so difficult? There is deep mystery here, and only when we are finally with God will we know the complete solution. Until then we must be satisfied with Christ's answer in today's Gospel: "Let both (weeds and wheat) grow together until the harvest; and at harvest time I will say to the reapers, Gather up first the weeds, and bind them in bundles to burn; but the wheat gather into my barn."

Our concern should be less about evil and men than with ourselves, with our nearness or farness from the ideal that Christ sets for us, the good grain. Death and judgment, final harvest, are for all — good and bad, weeds and wheat. Heaven is only for the good.

But an even greater concern should be for us to see to it that the weeds do not increase. Surely, when Christ said "Let them both grow until the harvest," He did not mean that we should be complacent about evil. He meant only that we must expect it, meanwhile being wide awake and active in our apostolic efforts to make the institutions of society in which we live as healthful and as conducive to salvation as possible. (It was while the householder's men slept that the enemy came and sowed the weeds in his field).

Our Lord wants us to know that there is a hell. And He wants us to fear it. The weeds will burn. And so shall we if we are faithless to our vocation, if we do not bring forth the fruit of holiness in ourselves and, in as far as possible, in others. But above all, our Lord wants us to know that there is a heaven and that He awaits us there. And thus we come to the second portrait of this Mass.

GOD'S CHOSEN ONES

We have seen the portrait before... on the Feast of the Holy Family. It is St. Paul's description of the ideal Christian community.

He treats first of all of the relations we should have one to another in this community: "Brethren, put on, as God's chosen ones, holy and beloved, a heart of mercy, kindness, humility, meekness, patience. Bear with one another and forgive one another, if anyone has a grievance against any other; even as the Lord has forgiven you, so also do you forgive. But above all these things have charity, which is the bond of perfection" (Epistle).

Then he goes on to the individual and public prayer life of the community as a whole and of its separate members: "Show yourselves thankful. Let the word of Christ dwell in you abundantly: in all wisdom teach and admonish one another by psalms, hymns and spiritual songs, singing in your hearts to God by his grace."

And finally, he gives the general motivation each member should have in all that he does: "Whatever you do in word or in work, do all in the name of the Lord Jesus Christ, giving thanks to God the Father through Jesus Christ our Lord."

CONNECTING REALITY TO IDEAL

It is an admirable picture that St. Paul gives of what the Church should be, and it makes us wonder if it will ever be realized. It would perhaps be better if we examined ourselves on whether or not we have ever tried to realize it in our families, our parishes, our schools... in ourselves.

But it is not only an ideal: it is a method of reaching the ideal that St. Paul gives us; it is a positive way of life. We are one with one another, we are all one in Christ. We are a community. We could spend our time worrying about weeds and occasionally plucking one out. And that is good. But what is better is for us to live, pray, work, sing, play together as a family, doing everything "in the name of the Lord Jesus Christ, giving thanks to God the Father through Jesus Christ our Lord." "O Lord, we beg Thee in Thy never-failing goodness, *to guard Thy family*, and since it depends entirely on the hope of Thy heavenly grace, defend it always by Thy protection" (Collect).

In that kind of family weeds cannot take root. In that kind of family all the members approach the final harvest together, but without fear, for it is made up of God's chosen ones, holy and beloved. Having lived, prayed, suffered together, the peace of Christ is their reward, for "unto that peace, indeed, they were called in one body" (Epistle). Having been true to their vocation as members of a holy community, they are the good wheat that will be gathered into the heavenly barns.

284

FOOD FOR THE WAY

1. Above all these things have charity which is the bond of perfection (Epistle).

2. Let the word of Christ dwell in you abundantly... singing in your hearts to God by his grace (Epistle).

3. Gather up first the weeds, and bind them in bundles to burn; but the wheat gather into my barn (Gospel).

TWENTY-FIFTH SUNDAY AFTER PENTECOST

(Sixth After Epiphany)

THE GROWING CHRIST

"The kingdom of heaven is like a grain of mustard seed, which a man took and sowed in his field... The kingdom of heaven is like leaven (yeast) which a woman hid in three measures of flour, until all of it was leavened" (Gospel).

Christ could as well have said: "I am like a grain of mustard seed that has been sown in the soil of this world... I am the yeast that is to penetrate and transform not only the souls of men, but the whole of their lives." Christianity is Christ. Christ is the Catholic Church, He is the kingdom of heaven. Christ grew rapidly in the soil of the world through the instrumentality of His apostles and the communities of Christians founded by these apostles. At Jerusalem, Rome, and elsewhere men tried to stop His growth, to root out this Seed. They might as well have tried to put a ceiling on the rise of the ocean's tide.

For Christ — Christianity — is a *divine Seed*, delivered to the world not only in word, but in power also. and in the Holy Spirit, and in much fullness (Epistle). Christ at Thessalonica, Christ in Rome, Christ in America, in Ireland, France, India, England, Germany, Russia. Christ then and now. It is the same Christ. He continues to grow. He can never be rooted out.

RETARDED GROWTH

But if Christ cannot be rooted out, His growth in men and society can be and is retarded. There are war, social injustice, racial hatred, greed, distrust, despair, and blindness to spiritual values on all sides... and all this in spite of the fact that Christianity is numerically more widespread today than ever before. Christ wants to be not only like a mustard seed spread by the wind. He wants to be like yeast that spreads interiorly, possessing men's souls, changing them into other Christs. And He wants these other Christs to become transforming yeast in their surroundings so that they will become a "pattern to all the believers in Macedonia and in Achaia... So that from them the word of the Lord will spread abroad in every place" (Epistle).

The world needs Christ, the divine Seed, the permeating Yeast. But often it cannot find Him where He is most to be expected: in the lives of His own chosen ones, in our lives. And He is not in our lives because we have not sought to share Him with our world. Someone has said that, if we cannot give what we do not have, so neither can we keep what we do not share.

Today we pray: "Grant us, we beseech Thee, O

Almighty God, ever to fix our thoughts on reasonable things and to *do what is pleasing to Thee both in words and in works*" (Collect). But what can be more pleasing to Him than the apostolate? "The kingdom of heaven is like a grain of mustard seed... It is like leaven hidden in three measures of flour."

The year is drawing to a close. As we glance back over it to see if we are closer to God now than when we began, we might also examine and weigh our efforts in the apostolate. Have we done anything at all? Have we prayed for the spread of Christ's kingdom? Have we sacrificed for it? Could we have done more, prayed more, sacrificed more? We must remember Daniélou's words: "Christianity is Catholic by definition, that is, it embraces the world. A Christian spirituality that is not fundamentally oriented toward the building up of the total Mystical Body is not a Catholic spirituality" *(The Salvation of the Nations*, Page 1).

THINGS BY WHICH WE TRULY LIVE

If our spirituality in the past has been self-centered, unconcerned about the kingdom of heaven being spread on earth, there is still time for it to be changed. Christ can do it. But we must cry out to Him: "From the depths I have cried to Thee, O Lord; Lord hear my prayer" (Offertory verse). How right for us to pray these words just before the offertory of the Mass!

For the Mass is the Sacrifice of Christ from which the mustard seed and the yeast received all its power. Since it is the sacrifice of Christ, it is the answer to every need that we and our world could possibly have. In it is our joy, our peace, our rest. In it is the true Christian spirituality that is fundamentally oriented towards building up the total Mystical Body. We can enter into that sacrifice, and when we do, we enter into direct relations with God.

We hold up bread and wine in offering. But what we really offer are our starving hearts. We hold them up so that God can fill them with Himself. Out of the depths we cry to Thee, O Lord. Hear our prayer. "Grant that we may ever hunger after those things by which we truly live" (Postcommunion prayer). Free us from selfishness and isolationism. "O God, grant... that we may be made partakers of His divinity who deigned to become partaker of our humanity, Jesus Christ Thy Son, our Lord" (Second Offertory prayer).

That prayer will not go unheard if it is prayed earnestly and sincerely. The Father in heaven answers it: "I think thoughts of peace, and not of affliction; you shall call upon Me and I will hear you; and I will bring back your captivity from all places" (Introit). God does what He says He will do. He hears our prayers at this and every Mass. But it is particularly at Communion that He will fill us with Himself. Out of the depths of human misery we cry to Him. Out of the depths of divine mercy and love He answers us. YOU SHALL CALL UPON ME, AND I WILL HEAR YOU.

The time is short. The harvest of judgment approaches. But if we turn to God, cry out to Him, fill our minds, our hearts, our wills with His apostolic mind, then we too will be Christ the Yeast, penetrating, transforming our communities.

289

1. You turned to God from idols, to serve the living and true God, and to await from heaven Jesus, His Son (Epistle).

2. This indeed is the smallest of all the seeds; but when it grows up it is larger than any herd and becomes a tree, so that the birds of the air come and dwell in its branches (Gospel).

3. May we ever hunger after those things by which we truly live (Postcommunion prayer).

LAST SUNDAY AFTER PENTECOST

THE VISION OF MOTHER CHURCH

Today at the end of the Liturgical Year Mother Church looks into the future. She sees "the Son of Man coming upon the clouds of heaven with great power and majesty" (Gospel). And she beholds the terrifying events that will accompany that coming.

Looking further she sees time running into eternity, and time, instead of marching on, trickles out and ceases to be. She catches a glimpse of the "today", the ever-lasting "now-ness" of God taking to Himself the puny centuries of years that He lent to the world. The high noon of the day that is eternity reigns over all.

In her vision Mother Church also beholds eternity gathering to itself the men who have lived in time... gathering them as they are, as they have lived. She hears Christ speak to the good in fulfillment of the pro-phecy of today's Introit: "I have brought back your captivity from all places." "Come, blessed of my Father, take possession of the kingdom prepared for you from the foundation of the world; for I was hungry and you gave me to eat; I was thirsty and you gave me to drink; I was a stranger and you took me in; naked and you covered me; sick and you visited me; I was in prison and you came to me... As long as you did it for one of these, the least of my brethren, you did it for me" (Matthew 25:34-41).

And she also hears Christ addressing the evil men: "Depart from me, accursed ones, into the everlasting fire which was prepared for the devil and his angels. For I was hungry and you did not give me to eat; I was thirsty and you gave me no drink; I was a stranger and you did not take me in; naked, and you did not clothe me; sick, and in prison, and you did not visit me... As long as you did not do it for one of these least ones, you did not do it for me" (Matthew 25:41-46).

THE REMEMBERING OF MOTHER CHURCH

So that is the end. Or is it? No, it is really the beginning, the commencement for the earthly, militant Church of that triumphant existence won for her by the life, death, and resurrection of Christ, her Head. She and we her children are redeemed because a Child was born to us whose government was upon His shoulder, a Child who was also a King, but a King who reigned from a cross, a King who died, who rose again, who ascended into heaven, who established a Church and chose us as members of that Church. Therefore she sums up her gratitude in these words of the Gradual: "Thou has delivered us, O Lord, from them that afflict us: and hast put them to shame that hate us. In God we will glory

all the day: and in Thy Name we will give praise forever."

In the face of Judgment, remembering all that God
has done for her and her children, Mother Church demands that we all "Give thanks to God the Father, who
has made us worthy to share the lot of the saints in light.
He has rescued us from the power of darkness and
transferred us into the kingdom of His beloved Son, in
whom we have our redemption, through his blood, the
remission of sins" (Epistle).

THE PRACTICALITY OF MOTHER CHURCH

With the vision of the future providing a salutary
fear and the remembering of the past giving confidence
and solid hope to us her children, the Church gets down
to the serious work of preparing us for the day when
vision will become actuality. For she knows that, although mankind as such is redeemed, we who make up
mankind can still be lost. She also knows that multitudes
of our fellowmen can be lost for want of our doing something for them.

First of all, Mother Church prays for us: "*Stir up
the wills* of Thy faithful people... so that the more
earnestly they seek the fruit of Thy divine service, the
more abundantly they will receive the remedies of Thy
mercy" (Collect). And again: "Be Thou gracious, O
Lord, to our humble appeals and, after receiving the offerings of Thy people, *convert the hearts of all to Thyself*, so that, having been set free from the greed of

earthly pleasures, we may pass on to the desire of heavenly treasures" (Secret prayer).

The world and its business are going up in smoke. And if the world and its pleasures have too great a hold on us, we will go up — or rather, down — with it. No man can serve two masters. We cannot serve God and mammon. God is our end. For Him we were made. Nor can our neighbors serve two masters. Is God, whom we claim to love, happy at the prospect of losing so many whom His Son gave His blood to save? STIR UP OUR WILLS... CONVERT OUR HEARTS!

Then the Church lectures us, reviewing all the things essential for our individual and corporate spiritual growth and development: "Be filled with the *knowledge of God's will* (How often during this year have we heard that!). May you walk worthily of God and please Him in all things, bearing fruit in every good work and growing in the knowledge of God. May you be completely strengthened through his glorious power unto perfect patience and long-suffering; joyfully rendering thanks to God the Father, who has made us worthy to share the lot of the saints in light" (Epistle).

The one way to know God's will and to do it, to walk worthily of God and to please Him in all things is by day-to-day fidelity to our vocation in life, to the little as well as to the great elements of that vocation. In our vocation we save ourselves. In fidelity to all its aspects we come to think as Christ thinks, we become like Him a living Yeast that leavens and sanctifies all with whom we associate. If the Son of Man coming in the clouds of heaven finds us working at our vocation, joyfully rendering thanks to God through it, we will not have to worry about His verdict. We will be ready for Him.

We are Christians, we are redeemed. And in this very Mass we are going to offer ourselves with, and we will receive in holy Communion, the same Christ who will one day judge us. We go away from His Mass knowing that the moment of His coming to us in glory is still uncertain; but at the same time we will be filled with a holy hope and a burning desire for Him that will carry us through any human discouragement. "In God we will glory all the day: and in Thy Name we will give praise for ever" (Gradual).

FOOD FOR THE WAY

1. I think thoughts of peace and not of affliction; you shall call upon me and I will hear you (Introit).

2. Heaven and earth will pass away, but my words will not pass away (Gospel).

3. From the depths I have cried out to Thee, O Lord: Lord, hear my prayer; from the depths I have cried out to Thee, O Lord (Offertory verse).

APPENDIX

IMPORTANT FEASTS

FEAST OF THE IMMACULATE CONCEPTION, DECEMBER 8

THOU ART ALL FAIR

It is our Blessed Mother herself who greets us in today's Introit: "I will greatly rejoice in the Lord, and my soul shall be joyful in my God; for He hath clothed me with the garments of salvation, and with the robe of justice He hath covered me, as a bride adorned with her jewels" (Introit).

She is describing the admirable privilege that God had conferred upon her in her Immaculate Conception. She, of all the daughters of men, could use these words of the prophet Isaias in fullest truth. God had "prepared a worthy dwelling place for His Son by preserving her from every stain of sin" (Collect). From the first moment of her being, she was filled with divine Life. That is what the Immaculate Conception means. And that is why the angel Gabriel could come to her and thus great her, "Hail, *full of grace*, the Lord is with thee. Blessed art thou among women" (Gospel).

Today the Church empties her treasures of praise in paying tribute to Mary in this festive celebration of her Immaculate Conception. "Blessed art thou, O Virgin Mary, by the Lord, the Most High God, above all women upon the earth. Thou art the glory of Jerusalem, thou art the joy of Israel, thou art the honor of our people. Thou art all fair, O Mary, and there is in thee no stain of original sin" (Gradual and Alleluia verses).

HOLY IS HIS NAME

And how does the humble maiden of Nazareth react to all the honor that is given her? "I will extol Thee, O Lord, for Thou hast upheld me: and hast not made my enemies to rejoice over me" (Introit). "My soul magnifies the Lord, and my spirit rejoices in God my Savior; because he has regarded the lowliness of his handmaid... because he who is mighty had done great things for me, and holy is his name" (Luke 1:46-49).

Mary always referred everything to God. He was her life. She lived for Him. The Lord possessed her from the beginning of His ways, before He made anything from the beginning (Epistle). She saw herself always and only as an instrument in God's plans. "Behold the handmaid of the Lord; be it done to me according to thy word" (Luke 1:38).

Mary's entire life was a breathing forth of the initial gift of her life into God's hands. That is prayer — the gift of self to God: living, working, acting under His guidance. The will of God entailed great pain for her. She stood beneath the Cross on Calvary, her heart pierced with the sword of grief. But God also brought her to the joy of her Son risen from the dead, to the Mount of His Ascension into heaven, and finally to her own glorious Assumption. "Be it done to me according to thy word," she had prayed; and so it was done.

GLORIOUS THINGS ARE SPOKEN OF THEE

Mary is our Mother; therefore she is concerned about us, about every aspect of our life, especially our prayer and apostolic life. Loving her Son as she did and does, she can hardly help being interested in those things we say and do that can best promote His glory. "Now, therefore, children, hear me: blessed are they who keep my ways... Blessed is the man who hears me, and who watches daily at my gates... He who shall find me shall find life, and shall have salvation from the Lord" (Epistle). The ways of Mary that she wants us to keep are the ways to God. "We pray that Thou wilt permit us to come to Thee, after being purified by her intercession" (Collect).

Miss Caryll Houselander writes beautifully of the way in which we can make the ways of Mary our ways: "It is Our Lady — and no other saint — whom we can really imitate... Each saint has his special work: one person's work. But Our Lady has to include in her vocation, in her life's work, the essential thing that was to be hidden in every other vocation, in every life. She is not only human, she is humanity. The one thing that she did and does is the one thing we all have to do, namely, to bear Christ into the world. Christ must be born from every soul, formed in every life... Nothing but things essential *for us* are revealed to us about the Mother of

298

God: the fact that she was wed to the Holy Spirit and bore Christ into the world. *Our crowning joy is that she did this as a lay person and through the ordinary daily life that we all live;* through natural love made supernatural, as the water at Cana was, at her request, turned into wine" *(The Reed of God,* p. xii, italics inserted).

Mary bore Christ into the world. She did this in her everyday life. That is what we too must do. Now we are in the Advent season. Already Christ is forming Himself in us. He will continue to grow in us during this year. But just as He did not come to Mary for her sake alone, but for the sake of the world, so He does not want to come to us just to satisfy our desires. To keep Him we must share Him, we must bring Him forth in our life, in our particular vocation. That is what the apostolate is: receiving Christ, growing in union with Him more and more, and then giving Him to others.

These are the ways of Mary, the ways that will give us the right to cry out with her: "My soul magnifies the Lord, and my spirit rejoices in God my Savior... because he who is mighty has done great things for me, and holy is his name."

FOOD FOR THE WAY

1. Thou art all fair, O Mary, and there is in thee no stain of original sin (Alleluia verse).
2. Hail, Mary, full of grace, the Lord is with thee. Blessed art thou among women (Offertory verse).
3. Glorious things are spoken of thee, O Mary; for He that is mighty hath done great things unto thee (Communion verse).

FEAST OF ST. JOSEPH,
MARCH 19

A JUST MAN

In such distinguished company as Jesus and Mary, St. Joseph necessarily takes an obscure place. That is the way he would have wanted it. But in the eyes of Mary and her Son, Joseph was far from obscure or unimportant. He was their guide and protector. He was the head of the family, "a just man, who was given by Thee as the spouse of the Virgin Mother of God, and as a faithful and wise servant was set over Thy family, so that with fatherly care he might guard Thy Only-begotten Son" (Preface).

Joseph did his work well — from the preparations for the birth of Jesus, through the flight into Egypt, to the quiet, hidden, laborious life of Nazareth. He was a worker, a carpenter. And we may well believe that he was a good worker and carpenter, that he was true to his worker's vocation every moment of his life. Being true to that vocation included teaching his foster-Son to be a worker, too, instructing Him by his own reverence for his tools and materials the dignity of cooperating with the Creator in making things that could be useful in the household.

At the end of his worker's life, his life of feeding, protecting, and providing for Jesus and Mary, he died in their arms. He asked "life of God, and God gave him length of days forever and ever" (Gradual). He passed on from being the head of the Holy Family of Nazareth to the equally distinguished dignity of being protector of the holy family of God spread throughout the world, the Mystical Body of Christ. "The just shall flourish like the palm-tree: he shall grow up like the cedar of Libanus: planted in the house of the Lord, in the courts of the house of our God" (Introit).

DO NOT BE AFRAID, JOSEPH

What made Joseph so great a saint? Fidelity to his vocation and living always in the presence of Jesus and Mary would, of course, make a saint of any man. But Joseph had the makings of a saint before he had any contact with them.

St. Matthew hints at the secret of his holiness. Upon noticing that his bethrothed was with child, "Joseph, her husband, being a just man, and not wishing to expose her to reproach, was minded to put her away privately. But when he thought on these things, behold, an angel of the Lord appeared to him in a dream, saying, 'Do not be afraid, Joseph, son of David, to take to thee Mary thy wife, for that which is begotten in her is of the Holy Spirit" (Matthew 1:19-21).

So Joseph was not only just, but also thoughtful and

charitable. He had complete trust in God, he never faltered in obedience to God's will. Therefore in him were fulfilled the words of the Psalmist: "Blessed is the man that feareth the Lord: he delighteth exceedingly in his commandments. His seed shall be mighty upon earth: the generation of the righteous shall be blessed. Glory and wealth shall be in his house: and his justice remaineth for ever and ever" (Tract).

HIS MEMORY IS IN BENEDICTION

Today we celebrate Joseph's feast. And how do we celebrate it? Not so much by extolling his virtues, but by praising God. It is to God that we offer this Mass, this "sacrifice of praise" (Secret prayer). "It is good to give praise to the Lord: and to sing to Thy Name, O Most High" (Introit). And so, even after all these years, Joseph teaches us the same values by which he lived: that God is everything, that praise and worship and service of God are above all other goods, and that this service of God is best fulfilled in the dedication of self to one's state in life.

But God does not let him go without his reward, this humble man who was "beloved by God and men, whose memory is in benediction" (Epistle). To the love of Jesus and Mary for him has been added the love and trust of millions of his sons and daughters of all times. "His seed is mighty upon earth."

Joseph is not gone from us any more than he was gone from Jesus and Mary. He was their protector. Their will was his will. Hence we may be certain that what was closest to their will — the coming of the Kingdom of God on earth — should continue to be his concern after he left this earth. He has been appointed the fatherly protector of the universal Church. Therefore he must be the fatherly protector of those who are seeking to make that Church more universal, those who are giving themselves to be used by God as His instruments for the intensifying and spread of His kingdom.

"We beseech Thee, O Lord, to help us through the merits of the Spouse of Thy most holy Mother so that *what we cannot obtain of ourselves* may be given to us *through his intercession*" (Collect). We shall want to remember that prayer the next time we find progress in the apostolate difficult. Which means that we shall want to remember it now and always.

FOOD FOR THE WAY

1. It is good to give praise to the Lord: and to sing to Thy Name, O Most High (Introit).

2. Blessed is the man that feareth the Lord: he delighteth exceedingly in his commandments (Tract).

3. Do not be afraid, Joseph, to take to thee Mary thy wife, for that which is begotten in her is of the Holy Spirit (Matthew 1:21).

FEAST OF SAINTS PETER AND PAUL, JUNE 29

O HAPPY ROME

"This day Simon Peter ascended the agonising cross. Alleluia. This day the keeper of heaven's keys went on his way to Christ with joy. This day the apostle Paul, laying down his head for the name of Christ, was crowned with martyrdom" (Magnificat antiphon).

We are celebrating the birth of Peter and Paul into their heavenly life after their years of apostleship on earth. It was a triumphant day for them and for the young Church; for their blood joined to the blood of their Master, became the seed of new Christians, even as by that blood they became the founders and fathers of a new and greater Rome.

"O Happy Rome! whom that most glorious blood
Forever consecrates while ages flow:
Thou, thus empurpled, art more beautiful
Than all that doth appear most beautiful now"

(Vespers hymn).

304

It is also a triumphant day for us who now enjoy the Faith that is the fruit of their labor and blood — for us who now seek by God's grace to continue the apostolic work they began. But along with the rejoicing at the triumph of these her Princes, the Church takes the occasion to drive home some important points for our work.

AS THE FATHER HAS SENT ME

We pray as follows in the Collect: "O God, who hast made holy this day with the martyrdom of Thine apostles Peter and Paul; grant that Thy Church may in all things follow the precepts of those from whom it first received the faith."

The precepts of those from whom we first received the faith... But nowhere in this Mass does the Church mention these precepts. (The Mass, incidentally, concentrates almost entirely on Peter — so much so that another Mass is celebrated tomorrow with emphasis on St. Paul).

But if these precepts are not explicitly outlined in the Mass, it takes no great insight to figure out that they must be the same that Christ Himself gave to the apostles. "A new commandment I give you, that you love one another: that as I have loved you, you also love one another. By this will all men know that you are my disciples, if you have love for one another" (John 13:34-35). "Come, follow me, and I will make you fishers of men" (Matthew 4:19). "As the Father hath sent me, I also send you" (John 20:21).

On his way to Damascus to persecute Christians,

Saul was struck down by Christ. "Lord, what wilt thou have me do?" he asked. And Jesus answered, "Arise and go into the city, and there it will be told thee what thou must do" (Acts 9:6). To love one another, to be fishers of men, to follow Christ, to go into the city, the country, the factories, the schools, the business and professional world *bearing witness to Christ* — these are the precepts that we pray God to give us the grace and strength to obey.

The grace, the character, the power of Baptism and Confirmation have come down to us across the centuries from the hands of the Apostles and because they were obedient to Christ's commands. And so also the other Sacraments; so the Church herself. We are their heirs. But what we have from them is ours only in trust. We must hand it on. We can say with St. Paul: "He whose power enabled Peter to become the apostle of the circumcised, enabled me to become the apostle of the Gentiles; and they recognized the grace God had given me. The grace God has shown me has not been without fruit: that grace remains with me always" (Gradual of the Mass of the Commemoration of St. Paul).

SON OF THE LIVING GOD

But above all we can say with St. Peter: "THOU ART THE CHRIST, THE SON OF THE LIVING GOD" (Gospel). Whom do men say that Christ is today? Some say that He did not even exist. Others say that He was a good man, a great social reformer. Many think He was an idealist whose ideas were all right once upon a time. (If He was merely a "good man", and a social reformer, then He did not rise again and then, according to St. Paul, our faith would be in vain).

But whom do we say that He is? With Peter we answer: "Thou art the Christ, the Son of the living God," with emphasis on the present tense. *He is now.* He lives in His Church, in us. We are doing His work. This conviction about Christ must become a daily frame of mind for us as it was for Peter and Paul. The more we grow in that conviction, the more we will strive to make Him a living God to our contemporaries. And then the more right we will have to hear Him say to us: "Blessed are you... and I say to you, that you are little Peters, little rocks, upon which I build my Church today. The gates of hell shall not prevail against her."

FOOD FOR THE WAY

1. Their sound has gone forth into all lands. And their words to the ends of the earth (Versicle and Response of Vespers).

2. Thou art the Christ, the Son of the living God ((Gospel)!

3. Thou art Peter; and upon this rock I will build by Church, and the gates of hell shall not prevail against it (Gospel).

ASSUMPTION OF THE BLESSED VIRGIN

THE KING HAS DESIRED HER BEAUTY

STAR OF THE SEA guiding us to an eternal harbor is Mary, our Blessed Mother. A refreshing pause in the summer heat is the Feast of her Assumption. It brings us face to face again with basic ideas and ideals for this life of ours that we may have momentarily forgotten. "O Virgin most prudent, whither goest thou, bright as the morn? All beautiful and sweet art thou, O daughter of Sion, fair as the moon, elect as the sun" (Magnificat antiphon).

Like the Ascension of her Son, Mary's Assumption lifts up our thoughts to our true home. She had chosen "the best part" (Gospel) and that best part she now enjoys forever. What is this "best part?" It is union with God. "Behold the handmaid of the Lord; be it done to me according to thy word" (Luke 2:38) — these words were her consent to the union God desired of her. Thenceforth she was one with Him at His conception in her womb, at His birth in poverty at Bethlehem, during His public life and beneath the Cross when Simeon's

308

prophecy was fulfilled in her: "Thy own soul a sword shall pierce" (Luke 2:35). But she was also one with Him at His resurrection and ascension. God could not wait long to reward that kind of abandonment. "The King greatly desired her beauty" (Gradual); and He took her to Himself, body and soul. She fell asleep one day and awoke to the songs of angels praising God for the Lady whom He had brought up from earth to be their Queen.

In all things she sought rest in the will of God, and now she abides in the inheritance of the Lord forever. "Mary has chosen the best part, and it will not be taken away from her" (Gospel).

OUR ASSUMPTION

The best part which she now enjoys is what this Feast guarantees for us, her children, but only on certain conditions.

First of all, we must celebrate the feast with heart-felt joy. "LET US ALL REJOICE IN THE LORD, celebrating a feast in honor of the Blessed Virgin Mary, for whose Assumption the angels rejoice and join in praising the Son of God" (Introit). We simply cannot sing, or even recite, those exhilarating words without experiencing wings in our hearts, wings that live and bear us upwards and onwards. We become light as we progress along another stage in that process of *transfiguration* which Christ is daily trying to achieve in us.

In the second place, we must receive Holy Communion as often as possible... and with Mary's spirit of self-surrender to God, a self-surrender that includes detachment from the things of earth. Even God cannot lift us up from the earth and give us a taste of Mary's and the angels' joy today if we insist on tying ourselves to this world's values by the strong bonds of sin. Communion is Christ's surrender of Himself to us. As we free ourselves from attraction to sin, we experience a little of Mary's self-surrender to Him; and then we know Communion even now as the beginning of our life with her and her Son.

The third way of earning our assumption is by our work in the apostolate. "Men of Galilee, why do you stand looking up to heaven?" the angels said to the apostles at Christ's Ascension. "This Jesus will come again" (Acts 1:11). They can say the same to us today. It is right and good that we should look up to heaven and long to be with our Mother and her Son. But we must merit our assumption as she did — by greater and greater union with the will of God showing itself in greater and greater efforts to bring souls to her Son — souls and institutions that are trophies of our love for Him.

DEVOTION TO MARY

Our Blessed Mother is taken up from us. But she is still with us, is still our Mother. "May the prayer of the Mother of God come to the aid of Thy people, O Lord, and although we realize that she has passed from us according to the fate of all human flesh, may we nevertheless feel that in the glory of heaven *she is ever interceding for us with Thee*" (Secret prayer).

Mary is our advocate, and she pleads for us whether we know it or not. But just as a mother is more pleased when her child asks for his needs, so will Mary heed our prayers more surely if we ask daily, continually, without ceasing. We must pray for the things we need, especially in the apostolate. But what we must plead for above all is the grace *to want to do God's will in all things as she did.* In the heat and pain of this life, in sickness, in health, in suffering, in death our willingness to say with Mary "Be it done to *me* according to Thy word" will be our salvation and the salvation of our world.

"Mary is taken up into heaven; the angels rejoice and, mingling their praises, bless the Lord" (Offertory verse). We must hold on to her. Some day through her prayers we will "be spared from all the evils that now threaten us" (Postcommunion prayer), and once again, "Gaudent angeli... the angels will rejoice."

FOOD FOR THE WAY

1. Let us all rejoice in the Lord, celebrating a feast in honor of the Blessed Virgin Mary (Introit).

2. Mary is taken up into heaven; the angels rejoice (Offertory verse).

3. Mary has chosen the best part, and it will not be taken away from her (Communion verse).

FEAST OF CHRIST THE KING, LAST SUNDAY IN OCTOBER

THE KING REIGNS

"Pilate said to him, 'Thou art then a king?' Jesus answered, 'Thou sayest it; I am a king. This is why I was born, and why I have come into the world' " (Gospel).

Then the soldiers put a crown of thorns on His head and arrayed Him with a purple cloak. And they kept coming to Him, saying: "Hail, King of the Jews!" When this was over He went out, carrying His own throne on His shoulders. He set the throne on the mountain and was nailed to it. He died and was buried. But the third day He rose again from the dead, to rule as King and "head of the body, the Church; he, who is the beginning, the firstborn from the dead, that in all things he may have the first place. For it has pleased God the Father that in him all fullness should dwell, and that through him He should reconcile to himself all things... making peace through the blood of his cross" (Epistle).

This is He of whom the prophets wrote: "He shall rule from sea to sea, and from the river to the ends of the earth. And all kings of the earth shall adore Him, all nations shall serve Him. His power is an everlasting power that shall not be taken away: and His kingdom, a kingdom that shall not be destroyed" (Gradual and Alleluia verses).

This is He of whom the angel Gabriel spoke: "The Lord God shall give to him the throne of David, his father: and he shall rule in the house of Jacob forever, and of his kingdom there shall be no end" (Magnificat antiphon).

THE KING STILL REIGNS

The throne is now an altar. The King is no longer visible to the eyes of His subjects, but we believe absolutely that He is there. He had said: "And I, if I be lifted up from the earth, will draw all things to myself" (John 12:32). He began drawing all things and all men to Himself already during His earthly life. He will continue to draw until His kingdom is filled, till all men have become His reverent subjects.

Before our Baptism we were subjects of the king of darkness; but now we belong to Christ. Now we are members of the kingdom of the Son of God's love, in whom we have our redemption. As members of that kingdom, we are members of one another. His Life is in us and is the living bond of unity between us all.

Today we members of the kingdom gather around the throne of our King. St. Paul, His messenger, tells us: "Give thanks to God the Father who has made us worthy to share the lot of the saints in light. He has rescued us from the power of darkness, and transferred us into the kingdom of his beloved Son, in whom we have our redemption through his blood, the remission of our sins" (Epistle). And we, Christ's subjects, do give thanks. We give God the *Eucharist*, the great thanksgiving of our King himself, and together with Him, we give ourselves in a renewal of our allegiance and loyalty to our King.

THE KING REIGNS FOREVER

The days of the kingdom in this world are ended. The King has returned in majesty and has separated His subjects from those of the king of darkness. And taking them with Him to His eternal kingdom, He has given them back to His and their Father. "The Lord shall sit a King for ever. The Lord will bless His people with peace" (Communion verse). Now in very fact He has finished the work His Father gave Him to do and has handed over to the divine Majesty "and eternal and universal kingdom; a kingdom of truth and life, a kingdom of holiness and grace, a kingdom of justice, love and peace" (Preface).

The members of that glorious kingdom are those who learned by sacrificing their own wills to mount the throne with Christ while they were on earth. They ate frequently of the "food of immortality" (Postcommunion prayer), they gloried in serving under the standard of their King, and did all in their power to advance His cause. Now they reign with Him, and gathered around the permanent heavenly throne, they sing for-evermore: "Worthy is the Lamb who was slain to receive power and Divinity and wisdom and strength and honor. To Him belong glory and dominion forever and ever" (Introit).

FEAST OF CATHOLIC ACTION

Our celebration of this wonderful feast is bound to make us wonder: If Christ is really the King of Kings, why is He not recognized as such today and served universally? M. Georges Bernanos had a good answer: "The present state of the world is the Christians' shame. The great unhappiness of this world, the great tragedy, is not that there are atheists, but that we are such indifferent Christians. We are sending the world to perdition, we are attracting the lightning of God's wrath."

The Feast of Christ the King has been appropriately called the Feast of Catholic Action. It shows us what God wants and what Christ came to do and how He accomplished His objective. It also shows how far our families, our parishes, our universal Church now are from achieving our King's ideals of unity, peace, brotherly love, and a passion for God's glory. This feast is a divinely inspired appeal to all Catholics to put away hatreds and prejudices that destroy Christ's unity in us and between us, and to cast off the sins and sinful inclinations that separate us from Christ.

Christ wants unity. For that He came. For that He gave His blood. Unity of all men in Himself, unity of minds, of hearts. To bring about that unity in himself and then in society must be the aim of every truly Catholic, Christ-like heart. Living as our King lived, that is, offering ourselves in our apostolate as "peace-making and immaculate victims on the altar of the Cross" (Preface) is the only way to establish the kingdom of Christ in ourselves and then to spread it among "all the families of nations, torn asunder by the wound of sin" (Collect).

The prophecy must be fulfilled: "Ask of Me, and I will give Thee the Gentiles for Thy inheritance, and the utmost parts of the earth for Thy possession" (Offertory verse). The fulfillment of that prophecy is in our hands, with the help of God. But we must first be convinced in our own minds that Jesus Christ is "King of Kings and Lord of Lords" (1 Timothy 6:15).

FOOD FOR THE WAY

1. His kingdom is a kingdom that shall not be destroyed (Alleluia verse).

2. Thou sayest it; I am a king (Gospel).

3. The Lord will bless His people with peace (Communion verse).

FEAST OF ALL SAINTS, NOVEMBER 1

HARVEST FESTIVAL

Close to the end of her year of benignity and grace, in the midst of her warnings and pleadings to us to prepare ourselves for the Parousia (Christ's coming in glory), the Church celebrates the Feast of All Saints. It is a Harvest Festival of joy in heaven and on earth. First of all, for the *Father* whom the little ones of earth so loved and trusted; for the *Son*, whose way to the Father they so faithfully chose to follow; for the *Holy Spirit* whose inspirations they so joyfully and fruitfully accepted; for the *Church* whose crown of success they are; and for *us*, their brothers and sisters here below, whose encouragement they will always be.

"LET US ALL REJOICE IN THE LORD, celebrating a feast in honor of all the Saints, in whose solemnity the angels rejoice and join in praising the Son of God. Rejoice in the Lord, ye just: praise becometh the upright" (Introit).

The Saints in heaven and we here on earth *belong to the same family.* "I am the vine, you are the branches,"

317

Christ can say to them as He can to us. The same Christ who is the Life of their souls is the Life of ours. We are all one with them and one with one another because we are all one with Christ, the LIFE OF SOULS.

In this family feast we rejoice at their victory over sin, while they intercede for us so that we may some day be with them in glory. "The souls of the just are in the hand of God, and the torment of malice shall not touch them: in the sight of the unwise they seemed to die, but they are in peace" (Offertory verse).

SECRETS OF SANCTITY

St. John once had a glimpse of heaven. He tells us about it in the Epistle, without, however, telling us much about their life with God. His census-taking of all those in the sight of the Lamb, clothed in white robes, holding palms, praising and glorifying God — all this is liable to leave us a little cold. Further on in the Apocalypse (from which this Epistle is taken) he warms up to his subject a little more: "Oh! How glorious is the kingdom in which all the Saints rejoice with Christ" (Magnificat antiphon)!

The point is that St. John knew that no matter how hard he tried, he could not measure heavenly joy with an earthly yardstick. But we know that the promises of Christ will be fulfilled: "Your reward is great in heaven" (Gospel). The Saints see God face to face. They enjoy God, infinite Source of all joy. They know Him and love Him. And in this knowledge and love all their earthly yearning for truth, love, and life are fully, eternally satisfied. Nor is there any fear that they will lose what they have. The souls of the just are in the hand of God... they are in peace.

Today's Mass does more than feed our speculation about heaven's joys, important as that is. It also reviews for us the way and means whereby we too can join our brethren in their glory. The saints were not unreal beings. They were men and women like ourselves. They lived the same kind of life and followed the same vocations. They had to work, study, overcome temptations, suffer.

But they were obedient to the invitation of our Lord in today's Alleluia verse: "Come to me, all you who labor and are burdened, and I will give you rest." They knew that they were powerless to achieve sanctity by their own power alone; so they went to Christ. They accepted His way of life, they cooperated with Him when by His daily Eucharistic Sacrifice He sought to work in them and make them victim-minded as He was.

It was this Eucharistic victim-mindedness that helped them live up to the ideal of the Gospel: to become really *poor in spirit, meek, pure of heart, patient, merciful, charitable.* Thus their religion became for them "a basic energy, permeating, transforming, shaping their lives," and enabling Christ to possess them wholly.

SANCTITY FOR US

All during the past year Christ has been asking us to become saints. Today, naturally, He emphasizes the invitation. The formula of sanctity for us is the same one that has had so much success in the past: "Come to Me." To decide to come to Christ — to come all the way, holding back nothing — that is what He asks us to do.

The one thing that stands in the way of sanctity for us is our self-will. This feast, and all the millions of holy lives that made it possible, is a great drama of human wills sacrificed, emptied of self, and identified with the will of God. And so it must be with us. If we would be saints, we must learn to take what is most precious to us — our will, our wanting this or that — putting it on the altar and saying to Christ: You do my wanting for me.

This is a hard thing to do, or rather, a hard thing to be sincere about; because Christ's wanting for us might include sickness, suffering, death for ourselves or our loved ones. It might include failure and opposition in the apostolate, even failure in our life's work. That is why becoming a saint is not the task of a few months or years, but of a lifetime. But giving our wills to Christ is the green light He needs in order to make saints of us. He does the rest, and this feast is evidence that He does very well.

LET US ALL REJOICE IN THE LORD, celebrating a festival day in honor of all the saints... There is one thing that we can will with all our hearts, confident that it is also the will of Christ. And that is our joyous tribute of praise to our God because of what He has done for our brethren the Saints in heaven and what He continues to do for us who are still on the way.

FOOD FOR THE WAY

1. Blessing and glory and wisdom and thanksgiving and honor and power and strength to our God forever and ever (Epistle)!

2. Fear the Lord, all ye His saints: for there is no want to them that fear Him (Gradual).

3. In the sight of the unwise they seemed to die, but they are in peace (Offertory verse).

ALL SOULS' DAY

THOSE WHO HAVE GONE BEFORE US

If we will not learn to sacrifice our self-will on earth,
purgatory's pain will teach us. The departed souls are
they who have "gone before us and who sleep in the
sleep of peace" (Canon of the Mass). They departed this
life attached to Christ the Vine, alive with His grace.
They are saved. But they still suffer, they are not yet
purified entirely, they are not yet with God as the Saints
are. Therefore they cry out: "Woe is me, O Lord, that
my sojourning is prolonged" (Vespers antiphon).

"From the depths I have cried to Thee, O Lord,
Lord, hear my voice" (Psalm 129:1). Thus do the poor
souls pray to God. But so also do they entreat us, their
brothers still on earth. From the depths of their suffering
they cry to us to help them by our prayers and good
works; for they cannot merit, they can only suffer and
wait.

So we cannot forget or neglect the poor souls. Some
day, if God is good to us, we will be holy souls, too, and
then their prayer will be ours. Prayerful charity to them
now is demanded by the very nature of the bond of
divine Life uniting us to them, to the Saints, and to

Christ. They are our brothers in the Communion of Saints. We can be assured that they will not forget us when they receive their intercessory powers after their sojourning in purgatory is over.

SWALLOWED UP IN VICTORY

All Soul's Day is not only an appeal to our charity. It also stimulates faith in the resurrection of the dead and hope that we too shall attain to that happy conclusion to our life. "We shall indeed rise again, but we shall not all be changed. In a moment, in the twinkling of an eye, at the last trumpet; for the trumpet shall sound, and the dead shall rise again incorruptible, and we shall be changed... And when this mortal hath put on immortality, then shall come to pass the saying, Death is swallowed up in victory... But thanks be to God, *who hath given us the victory through our Lord Jesus Christ*" (Epistle).

We can help the departed souls; but they in turn, in this commemoration, can teach and inspire us in the things that are truly necessary for us to know. In the light of what they have gone through, our Lord's words in the Gospel of the first Mass strike home with special force: "They who have done good shall come forth unto resurrection of life; but they who have done evil unto resurrection of judgment." There is no need for us to speculate on the choice our departed brethren would have us make.

For those who have no God (and even for many
Catholics who have not learned by prayer to cultivate
the sense of God's goodness) death is terrifying and
brutal. For them death has a finality that grieves the
depths of the human soul. But for those who know God
and love Him, for those who follow Christ's way of
trusting fidelity to God's will, death is but the beginning
of life. (At the cemetary, when a departed person is
about to be lowered into the grave, the priest quotes
Christ (John 11:25-26): "I am the resurrection and the
life; he who believes in Me, even if he die, shall live;
and whoever lives and believes in Me, shall never die").
By walking in God's presence their oneness with Christ
has become as real as death itself; and in that consciousness of union with Him "the hope of a blessed resurrection hath shone upon them: that those whom the cer-
tainty of dying afflicteth, the promise of future immortality may console. For unto Thy faithful, O Lord, life is
changed, *not taken away:* and the abode of this earthly
sojourn being dissolved, an eternal dwelling is prepared
in heaven" (Preface).

We are children of Adam and Eve, and therefore
we must die. But we are redeemed by Christ. We are
members of the holy Community that joins us to Him,
to the saints in heaven, and to the souls in purgatory.
Therefore we can cry out in all confidence: "Death *is*
swallowed up in victory. O death, where is thy victory?
O death, where is thy sting" (Epistle, First Mass).

The Church knows all this, even if we do not. As we

are carried out from our funeral Mass, she sends us on our way with one of the most joyous chants of her entire Liturgical treasure house: "May the angels lead thee into paradise: may the martyrs receive thee at thy coming, and lead thee into the holy city of Jerusalem. May the choir of angels receive thee, and mayest thou have eternal rest with Lazarus, who once was poor."

FOOD FOR THE WAY

1. Eternal rest give to them O Lord; and let perpetual light shine upon them (Introit).

2. Thanks be to God who has given us the victory through our Lord Jesus Christ (Epistle).

3. He who eats my flesh and drinks my blood has life everlasting and I will raise him up on the last day (Gospel, Third Mass).